1996

NEW DIRECTIONS FOR ADULT AND CONTI[N]

Ralph G. Brockett, *University of Tennessee, Knoxville*
Susan Imel, *Ohio State University*
EDITORS-IN-CHIEF

Alan B. Knox, *University of Wisconsin, Madison*
CONSULTING EDITOR

Facilitating Distance Education

Mark H. Rossman
Walden University

Maxine E. Rossman
Graduate School of America

EDITORS

Number 67, Fall 1995

JOSSEY-BASS PUBLISHERS
San Francisco

FACILITATING DISTANCE EDUCATION
Mark H. Rossman, Maxine E. Rossman (eds.)
New Directions for Adult and Continuing Education, no. 67
Ralph G. Brockett, Susan Imel, Editors-in-Chief
Alan B. Knox, Consulting Editor

Microfilm copies of issues and articles are available in 16mm and 35mm,
as well as microfiche in 105mm, through University Microfilms Inc., 300
North Zeeb Road, Ann Arbor, Michigan 48106-1346.

LC 85-644750   ISSN 0195-2242   ISBN 0-7879-9935-0

NEW DIRECTIONS FOR ADULT AND CONTINUING EDUCATION is part of The
Jossey-Bass Higher and Adult Education Series and is published quarterly
by Jossey-Bass Inc., Publishers, 350 Sansome Street, San Francisco,
California 94104-1342. Second-class postage paid at San Francisco,
California, and at additional mailing offices. POSTMASTER: Send address
changes to New Directions for Adult and Continuing Education, Jossey-
Bass Inc., Publishers, 350 Sansome Street, San Francisco, California
94104-1342.

SUBSCRIPTIONS for 1995 cost $48.00 for individuals and $64.00 for institutions, agencies, and libraries.

EDITORIAL CORRESPONDENCE should be sent to the Editor-in-Chief, Ralph
G. Brockett, Department of Educational Leadership, University of
Tennessee, 239 Claxton Addition, Knoxville, Tennessee 37996-3400.

Cover photograph by Wernher Krutein/PHOTOVAULT © 1990.

Manufactured in the United States of America on Lyons Falls
Pathfinder Tradebook. This paper is acid-free and 100 percent
totally chlorine-free.

CONTENTS

EDITORS' NOTES

The rapid rise in technology associated with distance education and learning is having a major impact on contemporary society. Computer-mediated instruction has created an entirely new vocabulary. The chapters in this issue are designed to help those concerned with facilitating distance education. They reflect the perspectives and concerns of the learner and the facilitator of learning in distance education settings.

In Chapter One, John Cantelon carefully develops a theme that is unique to distance education: its ability to transcend time and space. Reflecting on a career rich in distance learning experience, Cantelon sets the tone for the remainder of the issue.

In Chapter Two, Robert Stewart reviews the various technologies that are currently associated with distance education programs around the world. He also shares his view of future learning environments in which technology innovations are commonplace.

Chapters Three and Four are concerned with the human element in distance education programs. In Chapter Three, Waynne Blue James and Daniel Gardner urge the reader to consider learning styles in the context of distance education and discuss the critical need to recognize and facilitate individual learning styles. In Chapter Four, Dale Cook writes about the evolution of community and the need to develop a sense of community in the world of cyberspace.

Distance education as related to undergraduate and graduate programs is the focus of Chapters Five and Six. In Chapter Five, Gary Miller contends that one must understand and view the variety of practices in distance education as an agent capable of changing the undergraduate curriculum. Miller feels that despite its potential as a powerful agent of change, distance education practices and procedures have had little impact on the undergraduate curriculum. In Chapter Six, Craig Swenson concurs with Miller that distance education is a powerful agent of change and provides evidence of three graduate-degree-granting programs with markedly different delivery systems.

In Chapter Seven, Marlowe Froke describes the continuing education movement and urges distance education practitioners to learn from the past, particularly as it relates to issues of quality, costs, and the negative perception often associated with nontraditional education.

Chapter Eight presents information pertaining to distance learning resources. As an experienced reference librarian, Sherrill Weaver realizes that access to information is essential and provides pathways to find resources and information related to distance education.

Mark H. Rossman
Maxine E. Rossman
Editors

1

MARK H. ROSSMAN is professor of education at Walden University, Minneapolis, and a national specialization lecturer for Nova Southeastern University, Fort Lauderdale, Florida.

MAXINE E. ROSSMAN is dean for learner affairs at The Graduate School of America, Minneapolis.

Distance education has been with us for some time. It has the unique advantage of being able to transcend time and space.

The Evolution and Advantages of Distance Education

John E. Cantelon

This chapter is primarily an attempt to define what is unique about the kind of education that has come to be known, in North America at least, as distance education. In one sense, distance postsecondary higher education has been available since the nineteenth century. Indeed, the Chautauqua movement brought continuing education to millions of Americans long before anyone used distance education. In this century, those terms came to be applied to a wide variety of educational innovations that grew up in the varied but evanescent turmoil of the late 1960s' campus revolution. The word *nontraditional* was applied to the Berkeley-based Strawberry Canyon curriculum, nationwide teach-ins, and "days of concern" focusing on protesting the Vietnam War, and resulted in such widespread practices as putting students on almost all university committees, pass–fail courses, and increased course and faculty evaluation. *Distance education* was the term eventually used to describe radical educational experiments that transformed and spread to Antioch and led to such enduring experimental programs as Vermont College of Norwich University (1963), the Open University of Great Britain (1969), Walden University (1970), New College (1973), and the University Without Walls (1974).

Nontraditional education is increasingly identified with distance education or education taking place beyond the special spaces (campuses) traditionally set aside for such learning. The rapid development of computer networking capacity culminating in the Internet has encouraged and enabled distance learning to take place more effectively. No longer can distance education simply be referred to as education that takes place when there is a distance between the learner and instructor. In this definition, the distance being

NEW DIRECTIONS FOR ADULT AND CONTINUING EDUCATION, no. 67, Fall 1995   © Jossey-Bass Publishers

referred to is geographic, but distance might just as easily be cultural or emotional, with quite different pedagogical implications. One of the key characteristics of nontraditional higher education is the age of the students. Today, instead of the traditional undergraduate range of eighteen to twenty-three, more than 45 percent of college students are over twenty-five years of age and this percentage will continue to increase. The College Board predicts that the adult student population will be the fastest growing segment of higher education in the next century. This means that what has historically been defined as nontraditional will soon be the traditional-age cohort.

Emergence of Distance Education Programs

My interest in this form of higher education grew out of my experience as chair for two terms of the Senior Commission of the Western Association of Schools and Colleges during the period of intense experimentation in the late 1960s and early 1970s. In those days in California, the small liberal arts colleges such as LaVerne, Chapman, Golden Gate, and Pepperdine, followed by brand-new institutions such as National University and the University of Phoenix (which catered specifically to working adults) developed extensive off-campus programs both nationally and internationally. The motivation behind them was mixed. California was experiencing one of its periodic adjustments in the aircraft and defense industry. Building up or downsizing these industries created the need for new skills by mid-career professionals and both created new opportunities. It was also a time in which the small liberal arts colleges, many of them church-related, faced another of their many post–World War II fiscal trials and the off-campus, nontraditional programs were initially perceived as substantial money makers; they continued to be so to a more limited degree even after the regional accreditation associations insisted that off-campus programs be of comparable quality to on-campus programs.

From the beginning, these programs were hybrids, possessing characteristics of both traditional programs and nontraditional elements. In order to be evaluated by their home departments and to meet accreditation requirements, these programs were patterned after the campus-based curricula, but were nontraditional in terms of their compressed schedules, the older age and part-time nature of the students, and the extensive use of part-time instructors. They also tended to be restricted to the social sciences (particularly in business and public administration and the humanities) because of the difficulty of providing at a distance the laboratory and studio requirements of the natural sciences and the arts. The saving rationale for providing these programs was that they met the higher educational needs of vastly underserved constituencies (working professionals, the military, and minorities), all of whom found residence requirements unusually burdensome or impossible because of work and family commitments. They were also uniquely adapted to meet growing needs to provide continuing education for professional certification, licensure, and career advancement.

Characteristics of Nontraditional Distance Education

In order to answer the question once posed to this writer by Daniel Boorstin, then Librarian of Congress—"What is essentially nontraditional about nontraditional education?"—it is necessary to note some of the differences between these programs and those that went before. One of these differences was the age of the participants. College education traditionally has been available to eighteen- to twenty-three-year-olds, whereas the nontraditional programs were designed for those who had completed their undergraduate degrees and already had jobs, families, and community responsibilities. The trend to address the educational needs of older young adults had already been established by the impact of veterans returning to campuses to begin and complete the education interrupted by World War II and the Korean conflict. The GI Bill and its contemporary counterparts in such programs as the Pell Grants have made possible American world preeminence in higher education, particularly at the graduate level. At the same time, the development of the nontraditional segment of American higher education has enabled it to extend and expand two of its most important characteristics: availability and diversity.

Higher education's abandonment in the 1970s of one of its inherited primary functions of being in loco parentis changed far more than residence hall regulations. The lowering of the age of adulthood from twenty-one to eighteen deprived college education of its role of facilitator of the coming of age. Anthropologists noted that coming of age rituals often involved the temporary residency of the initiates outside of their homes in separate communities where, under the tutelage of a specially prepared cadre of elders, the young were introduced by mystic rites and ceremonies into the lore of the culture, after which they could then be welcomed back as fully recognized participants in the tribe.

I recall sharing with the master of Brasenose College at Oxford that the University of Southern California had just completed a review of admissions to the College of Letters, Arts, and Sciences for the past decade. He conveyed that they also had completed a similar review of admissions to Brasenose, but for the past 400 years, and found that one of the major differences between sixteenth- and twentieth-century undergraduates was their age. In the late middle ages, most college students were ages nine to fifteen, changing to what we regard as the traditional age grouping of eighteen to twenty-three only in the nineteenth and twentieth centuries. As we move into the twenty-first century, formal higher education will encompass a much wider age span than ever before in human history. As noted above, in the new millennium older students will constitute the majority of all students and most of higher education, at least in part, will take place off-campus in a university without walls.

The traditional walls that surrounded the medieval university (often surmounted by vicious-looking broken glass) have gradually become more symbolic than physically protective, as may be seen in the charming serpentine brick wall of Thomas Jefferson's University of Virginia. (We leave unaddressed the question of whether the walls were primarily designed to protect town from gown or gown from town. Probably both!) But perhaps the most decisive change in higher education in the 1990s has been the emergence of the university without walls. Modern communications systems have made it possible to overcome the stern requirement of geographic propinquity as an absolutely essential feature of higher education. Henry David Thoreau won his argument with the president of Harvard to the effect that the invention of the railroad had destroyed the rationale for the strictly local library borrowing privileges imposed by the university, just as the invention of printing had made it unnecessary to continue chaining books to the walls. Microfiche and computer data bases have modified and even transcended the spatial limitations imposed by library buildings and facilities.

Peter Drucker, in a speech at the USC faculty club, noted that faculty had been tremendously inventive of ways to avoid the positive impact technology could have on education. He suggested that faculty had managed, through their reliance on the lecture method of imparting information, to nullify successfully the impact of Gutenberg's invention of printing for 400 years! As faculty perhaps intuitively senses, a university without walls quickly becomes one in which the lecture method is made obsolete or, at the very least, radically transformed. Although laboratories and studios for the performing and fine arts may continue to be needed, the formal space of the large lecture hall will have limited utility in the future. For the social sciences and humanities, the most appropriate venue for teaching and research is the world beyond the campus. This is particularly true for the advanced-degree applied research that characterizes many distance education institutions.

One of the major obstacles to distance education has been the matter of providing library resources to dispersed students and faculty. It has been observed that a university is, simply and fundamentally, the interrelationship between three elements: the faculty, students, and a library. Since the eighteenth century, laboratories would have to be added along with the library. Of these three essential elements, the library more than the others forced the university to settle down in a particular physical location. The precursors of the university in the West lay in the peripatetic schools of the Greek philosophers, whose favorite meeting place was in the Athenian groves of Academe. So higher education began with the Greeks walking and talking in the woods, received institutional identity among the constantly migrating tribes of Islam, finally settled down behind walls of Christendom where the monks kept their precious manuscripts and, until the advent of nontraditional higher education, has been campus-bound ever since it leapt the Atlantic.

Before the establishment of Papua, Bologna, Paris, or Oxford, students had already taken the initiative to attach themselves to wandering clerics who later brought university administration into existence in order to free themselves for their teaching responsibilities. The informal living together by language groups of wandering students from all over medieval Europe in certain areas of town gave rise to the term *university* for those gathered in a specific location with the single objective of learning. The scarcity of books before the invention of printing limited the number and location of universities. It is only in our modern era, with the impact of communications technology, that the limitation represented by library collections has been overcome. First there was the miniaturization impact of microfilm and microfiche and then the computerization of card catalogs, accompanied by the creation of huge data bases and now the growth of the Internet. Scholars from all over the world today are interrelated on a daily basis as never before. This accomplishment has made a reality out of what was only a dream or vision from the Middle Ages to the present: the universal company of scholars.

Regional accrediting associations and state licensing boards have rightly raised questions about the lack of readily available library access on the part of distance education students and faculty. Simply turning students loose on the existing community and university libraries made the distance learning institutions appear parasitic and predatory. The argument often used by the nontraditional programs that their students are citizens and taxpayers and therefore due access to publicly supported libraries has only limited validity. It became obvious that the nontraditional institutions need to do more than just turn their students loose to fend for themselves as far as library resources are concerned. In the late 1970s, Central Michigan University's (CMU) distance learning program, the Institute for Personal and Career Development, pioneered nationally in providing library resources by hiring regional librarians, providing its 15,000 part-time students with toll-free 800 numbers and twenty-four-hour turn-around service from its Mt. Pleasant campus library. CMU also put on several national conferences sharing information on how to serve the distance learner.

As Edward Garten and Cynthia Hartwell noted in a report that encourages more collaboration between libraries and distance learning programs, "the intent of the regional accreditation bodies is that those individuals who propose offering academic work in remote or off-site fashion be especially responsive to the ways and means through which they provide learning resources to their students. When institutions are using the locally held resources of others, evidence of formal contracts, letters of understanding, and other documentation is being given increased attention" (1994, p. 91).

Triumph of Time Over Space

The task still remains to define the essence of nontraditional education in the short time provided by what were to be brief remarks at a graduation. It is like the challenge to Rabbi Hillel to define Judaism while standing on one foot! However, it can be argued that there is an essential element that characterizes nontraditional or distance education and it is one that can be traced back to the mainstream of Western philosophic thought. It involves wrestling with such abstractions as time and space. Human existence—indeed all existence that we know of—entails both time and space. Modern cosmology considers time and space to be inextricably interrelated. We measure time by space and we measure space by time, earthly years by rotations of our planet around the sun and sidereal space by the time it takes light from the spatially distant galaxies to reach us. (When you think of it, astronomers have always engaged in distance learning!) Space and time exist in a perpetual tension. To have space is to perdure, or to endure over a period of time. We measure time by spatial relationships, whether we talk about revolutions of the earth, the relationship between the stars, or the positions of hands on a clock.

Paul Tillich asserted that time and space constitute "the most fundamental tension of existence. In the human mind, this tension becomes conscious and gets historical power. Human soul and human history . . . are determined by the struggle between space and time" (1959, p. 30).

Tillich derived this particular insight from his study of the contrast between ancient space-bound pagan religions, with their highly localized deities and holy places, and the Jewish, Christian, and Islamic traditions with their omnipresent God who is lord of space and time.

A more recent example of the tension between space and time may be seen in our own national historical experience. America as a national entity exists only because of the triumph of time over space. Were it not for the rapid movement of the frontier across the great geographical spaces of this continent and the Pacific Ocean, this republic would either not have existed or would have taken quite a different form. Today's technological society depends on rapid communications and fast travel, both of which demonstrate the triumph of time over space. Thanks to modern achievements in communications, we are becoming what Marshall McLuhan called the global village.

One of the most severe problems faced by the former Soviet Union provided a startling example of what happens when space triumphs over time. The great distances involved in bringing crops to market and the failure of the Soviet system to create an efficient transportation system threatened to create a famine. The rise of ethnic groups, pressing for independence all over the world, from the Palestinians to the Bosnian Muslims also illustrates the space–time tension and reveals the triumph of spatial demands for territory and independence, which are at odds with what the times appear to call for in terms of a world tolerant of ethnic pluralism, cultural diversity, and human reconciliation. About the only areas in which it may be appropriate for space to be victorious over time are in the interrelated problems of population control and global ecological responsibility.

The so-called traditional university also provides further examples of the tension between time and space. Historically, the university consisted of a space–time equilibrium based on an agricultural society. The green campus quadrangle, with or without walls, enclosed a particular space set aside for the purposes of what was called higher learning. Still, in the minds of many, a university is primarily a physical location. Most think of college in physical or spatial terms: a plot of land on which sits a library, a chapel, and an Old Main. Indeed, for most of the twentieth century, higher education has been afflicted with what has been called an edifice complex, investing a very large percentage of its available funds in buildings and their maintenance. How much time and money could be saved if education were conducted with a view to fostering the victory of time over space demands while recognizing the legitimacy and need to strike some balance between them?

From Place to Process

What has been called nontraditional education depends on this balance being struck closer to the time end of the spectrum than the space side. Distance education allows for the application of time-sensitive self-paced learning and makes possible continuous registration and new forms of instruction freed from lockstep term or semester constraints. It respects individual learning styles, schedule differences, family responsibilities, and professional commitments. Distance learning has been immensely facilitated by air travel and computer networking. Education is no longer limited to the traditionally "proper" space of the classroom. A competency-based curriculum is essentially time-oriented rather than space-oriented. Nontraditional education is more centered around students' schedules; asynchronous telenetworking accommodates individual faculty schedule demands as well. Gone is the need for a uniform lockstep curriculum geared to the learning speed of the so-called average student. Time rather than space rules.

Traditionally, classrooms also involved carefully controlled spatial structures with raised platforms to support the professorial podium. Distance was established between the instructor and the student, as contrasted to the more informal seminar atmosphere of nontraditional programs and the cyberspace of electronic networking, where physical distance is but a computer screen away.

Distance education still involves the use of some spaces for learning, but what distinguishes them from the traditional education is that space does not dominate. What is truly unique about distance education is the site of learning is transformed from a place to a process. As the *On-line Chronicle of Distance Education and Communication* aptly put it, "In the Industrial Age we go to school. In the Communication Age, schools come to us."

These assertions are made by one who has as deep an appreciation as anyone for the traditional spaces associated with higher education, represented by the dreaming spires of my alma mater Oxford. Some parts of education should and will be space-specific. One could argue that the functions of *paidea* and *techne* require some form of physical propinquity, so that undergraduate education is best conducted on campuses. But graduate education, particularly in the social sciences, is best conducted in the hands-on, real-world settings used by nontraditional, distance education institutions.

Conclusion

In his report for the Minnesota Higher Education Coordinating Board, Dr. Helmut Schweger reviews developments in nontraditional education under a number of headings. He writes that it has moved from correspondence, home, and independent study to open learning. The latter term describes the rich variety of pedagogical forms, techniques, and strategies that have supplemented the traditional lecture method, which so long dominated traditional higher education. It includes the opportunities presented by modern communications technology to facilitate multimedia instruction. This has moved the faculty from playing question-and-answer experts and podium performers to being fellow students and facilitators of a wide variety of learning experiences. Schweger concludes his comprehensive review of higher education experimentation with the observation that distance education and open learning fill a void in the postsecondary education infrastructure by serving the unmet needs of new student populations. Distance education complements, rather than diminishes, the importance of colleges and universities.

References

Garten, G. and Hartwell, C. "Adversaries or Colleagues? The Nontraditional Entrepreneurial University and the Challenge Posed to Library Administrators." *Library Administration & Management,* 1994, 8 (2).

On-line Chronicle of Distance Education and Communication, Dec. 1994, 1 (7).

Schweger, H. "Open and Distance Learning, Alternative Approaches to the Delivery of Post-Secondary Education, an Identification of Trends, a Discussion of Issues, and a Review of Models." Discussion paper prepared for the Minnesota Higher Education Coordinating Board, Nov. 1994.

Tillich, P. *Theology of Culture.* Oxford: Oxford University Press, 1959.

JOHN E. CANTELON *is chancellor of Walden University, Minneapolis.*

The technology that supports distance education is complex. In the future, it can only grow.

Distance Learning Technology

Robert D. Stewart

The printed word is the most obvious and dominant medium used to transmit information whatever the context. This is no different in distance education settings. Verduin and Clark (1991) write that "print has always been the dominant medium in distance education and will continue to be the most used form of delivery in the foreseeable future" (p. 81). However, with the advent of technology, the diverse ways in which the printed word is transmitted are almost impossible to list. It is the intent of this chapter to provide a glimpse into several technologies currently associated with distance education.

Current Technologies

There are a number of distance-learning technological environments. Among these are the microwave broadcasts of both audio and video. These broadcasts of classroom learning modules are sent to remote learning sites equipped with receiving dishes. The distance is limited to a 25–50-mile range and the student interaction is limited to audio through a phone connection back to the broadcasting classroom. Such broadcasts are picked up by satellite for more remote locations, but then there is no interaction by the learners.

In the broadcast classroom situation, there is normally a single camera in the room, concentrating on the instructor or an experiment or the blackboard where notes are being written.

In other interactive distance learning setups, large-capacity, heavy-traffic T-1 phone lines provide two-way audio and video between the broadcast classroom, from which the educational materials and instruction originate, and the remote classroom. Effectively, a conference call is established between the sending and receiving sites and the analog signal connects them. Whatever the

New Directions for Adult and Continuing Education, no. 67, Fall 1995 © Jossey-Bass Publishers

focus of the camera (the instructor in the case of the primary broadcast classróom or the learners in the remote classroom), all parties can see each other and questions can be delivered at will to the instructor. The two-way direct line audio-video conferencing of this model is costly due to the need for a dedicated T-1 line or the newer, even more costly fiberoptic lines. These high-capacity, high-speed transmission lines connecting the sites are necessary due to the large quantity of digital material being transmitted. Most programs today use the first model, adding microwave broadcast with one-way video and a synchronous two-way audio connection.

All models still rely heavily on printed material sent ahead to the remote sites and asynchronous communication through e-mail and fax. Video recordings of appropriate learning modules are often provided for students who are unable to attend the remote classes.

Television has been used for distance learning since the early 1960s. The availability of VHS recordings has made this an even more popular mode of delivery. The video system of delivery, through standard television channels or mail delivery to the home, started the digital distance learning revolution. Instructional Television Fixed Service (ITFS) is a low-cost microwave transmission that uses line-of-sight stations placed approximately 20 miles apart. Satellite delivery systems have become more popular in the last few years with NASA's applications technology satellite series. The next-generation NASA satellites are designed to handle five times the number of transmissions than those currently available, including high-speed data transmission.

However, ITFS and satellite-delivered video signals are one-way transmissions. To more closely emulate the traditional classroom full interaction is necessary, and two-way full-motion video is required. Coaxial cable can provide such coverage, but fiberoptics is the wave of the future. A fiberoptic cable the size of a quarter in diameter can carry 50,000 simultaneous phone transmission links or hundreds of the more costly video signals when compression technology is used. To handle the expected increases in the telecommunication demands of the next century, fiberoptic data transmission lines, like telephone lines, are being laid underground in most major metropolitan cities in the United States. The major communication providers are connecting businesses, hospitals, colleges, and schools.

The long-term plan is to replace all standard copper wire lines with the new optical cables. In this form of cable, data signals can travel at the speed of light.

In videoconferencing, or two-way video distance learning, up to 30 frames per second (the standard for full-motion video) must be transmitted. One minute's worth of these digitized pictures takes up 15 megabytes of space. If the video could be compressed, it could be transmitted more rapidly.

Pending the availability of fiberoptics, major universities and school districts throughout the country remain wired for the Integrated Services Digital Network (ISDN), which uses compression technology to transmit voice, video, and data simultaneously over standard, twisted-pair telephone lines.

What Is Being Used Now

The California Community College Chancellor's Office Teleducational/Telecommuting Centers grants look for multiple-platform networks (those that connect UNIX, DOS, and Apple-type computers to a central file server with printing, telecommunications, and fax capabilities). The network connecting telecommunication system consists of at least fifty lines, an Internet access, and access to services such as InfoNet and CAVEX. It should conduct the classroom modules and videoconference meetings through a single analog telephone connection that carries both voice and the video data signal. Effectively, this means that digital information such as text, pictures, and sound, in digitized computer format (.wav files or video, saved as computerized .avi files), could be sent from a computer over a special modem that splits the signal into a voice channel and a data channel. Participants could talk simultaneously, interacting with all others hooked up to the analog telephone connection.

The California Community College system requires ISDN or high-speed data lines and would support videoconferencing. The video standard of H.320 is maintained with a still-image video file and compression standard of JAPG (the motion standard would be NPEG). The audio-graphic standard would be set to T.120 and full duplex. Each broadcast classroom would be equipped with CLIE clips that maintain full duplex (two-way) audio through multiple ISDN connections. The single connection only allows a minimum 112 kilobytes per second, whereas the multiple connections increase the resolution to 384 kilobytes per second. Each classroom would have two video cameras, a 486 computer with presentation and multimedia software installed, a scan converter for converting the computer signal to NTSC video signal, a VCR and laser-disc layer, a multiple bank CD-ROM, a telephone, and a special high-speed modem.

The Maryland Center for Public Broadcasting has constructed a video network linked with two local community colleges through a T-1 telecommunication backbone. Because of the carrying capacity of this line and the availability of compressed video, they can handle four simultaneous video signals, with room remaining for voice and data transmission. That means that the instructor, the blackboard, and some students can be seen on the screen at one time with full interactive capabilities.

Utah State University's Life Span Education Program links 30 sites using an audio-graphic system and EDNET 2, a compressed, digital, two-way, interactive video network. As Susan Douglas points out, many school districts and state educational offices are coming together to investigate the emergence of this new technology. "The metamorphosis taking place in transmission technology is also exemplified in the new, more powerful interactive technologies available for education programming and information storage. With the introduction of 'video dial tone' and interactive television just around the corner, colleges and universities are considering how to move the latest technology from the dorm room to the classroom. . . . The public broadcasting system has recently announced its decision to experiment with two-way television early next year" (1993, p. 29).

With the newer, faster communication links, two-way communication is possible and even cost-effective. A television signal can be sent from a classroom delivering a lecture-type course module and the students could call in on video phones to ask their questions and interact.

In the simpler, nonnetworked type of distance education, communication can occur through large educational research networks, through asynchronous (one-way at a time) e-mail connections, or through live, real-time telecomputing.

The Internet is a well-used medium for distance education, but there are hundreds of other networks throughout the world. In Canada, School Net connects more than 300 schools initiated by the Industry of Science and Technology, The Net (a new name for Envoy-100), and a number of other large educational networks. For classroom communication, distance learning models like those in Canada and with teachers such as Indu Varma of the Marshview Middle School of Sackville, New Brunswick, get to communicate directly and e-mail friends in Chile, Costa Rica, the United States, Germany, and Belgium. "The real power of telecommunication lies in bridging barriers of language, culture, distance, race, or religion and building ties that would otherwise be difficult to create" (Varma, 1993–1994, p. 373).

In the community college system of Maine, interactive television (ITV) is used successfully to harness the educational needs of dispersed and thinly populated groups of students. At the Community College Headquarters is a master control facility. The computers transmit data over a fiberoptic network to each campus hub through the audio–video router and digital connect switchers. At each campus, there is an audio–video router to switch electronic channels of fiberoptic digital lines between campuses. The ITV system provides video and audio interactive classes and special educational events. Each campus has the capability of transmitting the point-to-point microwave transmissions. Each campus hub can broadcast a one-way video and audio line-of-sight transmission signal from its own or another campus through the network that links sixty high schools, university centers, and technical colleges. Each site has two classrooms equipped with large-screen receivers, VCR, and cordless phones. Telephones are used to call the originating classroom with discussion questions. With multiple toll-free telephone lines into each classroom, multiple sites can simultaneously hear each other and interact with the instructor and other students in the electronic classroom.

In Australia, the problems of distance education hinge on small groups of potential students in very remote areas. Students are clustered whenever possible. The simplest distance learning link is a telephone conference call between the classroom and remote students. Speaker phones and microphones were used and hardcopy documents were faxed. To provide visual interaction in Queensland, Australia, a program called Electronic Classroom was installed in Macintosh computers. This provided an electronic chalkboard through modem-linked Macintoshes. Not only could text be transferred, but also full-color scanned images or simulations and video access was available through CD-ROMs and compressed video clips.

At NOVA University, a university without walls in Ft. Lauderdale, Florida, their electronic classroom (ECR) links a faculty member with groups of students at diverse locations, using individual computers and modems connected to a host computer creating the equivalent of a bulletin board chat mode. NOVA University's main frame computer uses the Internet and a UNIX operating system for the delivery of their instructional system. As Mizell and Carl describe it, "the ECR classroom is a 'virtual classroom'; it emulates the features of a regular classroom . . . the screen is divided with 16 lines at the top reserved for the instructor's 'blackboard.' The next four lines are the student's display window. . . . Students can 'raise their hands' by hitting a couple of keys. . . . There is even a four-line bumper available to all students for writing on privately" (1994, pp. 91–92).

When visual material is necessary, videotapes are sent to the distant learners before class so that the ECR session can concentrate on discussion. This simple system uses the personal computers of students and faculty, the Internet, and a central transfer point (NOVA's mainframe).

In the K–12 school arena, many networks in the United States provide the channel for distance learning communication. The FrEdMail Network, the National Geographic Kids Network, and the AT&T Learning Network are three of the largest. The FrEdMail Network is like the Internet and has a wide group of participants. The National Geographic Kids Network offers more specific project activities and curricula prepared by the National Science Foundation and National Geographic Society. The AT&T Network uses the concept of learning circles, where four to seven participants are assigned and a coordinator-mentor offers assistance and guidance. Through these and other networks, K–12 schools can access other schools in the United States and abroad to communicate through the computer and modem.

In an effort to provide media access to a large number of remote locations, Ball State University in Muncie, Indiana created a video information system in 1989, using a campuswide fiberoptic media network. One hundred eighty remote locations with control panels have direct access to a media distribution center and each remote location operates as many as six different media channels to provide high-tech education in the remote centers. The key to the dissemination of full-motion video to these remote centers is the fiberoptic network. The output has grown to 300 campuses and remote campus distribution points. VHS tapes, video stills, CD-I (compact disk interactive), 16-mm film, and 35-mm slides are piped through to the remote classrooms. Additionally, multimedia interactive learning modules are available. Beatty and Fissel report that "although other universities and many K–12 schools have followed Ball State's lead by installing integrated information systems of their own, the University's 300 room, 40 building network remains the largest and most complex of any in the nation, directly effecting over 2,500 students daily" (1993, p. 82).

Technological Future

The history of distance education has fallen short in the area of interaction. Without student interaction and greater access to information and other tools, the student is at a disadvantage compared to students in an on-campus educational model.

Sphnepf, Masheyekahi, Reidl, and Du state: "The present environment provides limited support for human–human interaction over distance and time, and suffers from a lack of appropriate tools for manipulating information" (1994, p. 21).

Miller and Clouse similarly feel that "productivity demonstrates distance education's capacity of providing simultaneous instruction to large numbers of students at a cost lower than incurred in traditional instructional delivery" (1993–1994, p. 194).

A survey of educators reveals the main areas of concern in the development of this new educational media. Miller and Clouse claim that the educators "explain that the interactive capabilities of technology, sharing of expert instructors, and professional course development insure quality distance education" (1993–1994, p. 194).

In the area of technology video has begun to emerge as a key element. Verduin and Clark (1991) state that we must "use digitized T.V. signals which, being 'compressed,' take up less room in a signal, allowing the carrying of additional audio and data signals that may pay the cost of the video portion" (p. 71).

If distance education is to prosper in the coming decades, an increase in the level of interaction has to occur in the support services available, such as libraries and learning resource centers, and interactive student discussion groups. One-on-one interaction with faculty must be improved. With the injection of fiberoptic communication lines with hundreds of times greater transmission capabilities than T-1 phone lines, the path is open for increasing the amount of interaction and providing the support services necessary to round out distance education. Current hardware technology exists and software is being written for a full two-way audio–video link between the broadcast classroom with all remote students, be they in remote classrooms situated in the remote surrounding areas or, through direct satellite link and fiberoptics, using interactive home computers. Imagine the screen splitting from only the instructor and the blackboard or experiment at hand to a student asking a question to five or six other students joining the group discussion. At present, this technology exists in a K–12 environment in the Global Schoolhouse in Carlsbad, California. Yvonne Andes' students communicate via live audio–video signals with students in other countries around the world through the Internet.

In the distance learning model of the future, ancillary materials mailed to distance education students in the past should give way to online data bases and audiovisual interactive tutorials, texts, and graphics made available by the instructor or course originator. These reference and tutorial materials would be available on workstations in remote classrooms or available for the home computer user to access, much like an online service or bulletin board of today. With the greater transmission capacities of fiberoptics, full-motion video, audio, and multimedia of all forms could be added to the available resource materials piped directly to the student in an interactive, on-demand basis, adding a self-paced element to the learning module. These materials would be collected by the instructor into a centralized location available to the remote student in order to limit the information overload of available resources and the sorting and search refinement that would be necessary to guide the student through the vast library of resources. In this distance education scenario of tomorrow, the remote learner would have access to the instructor through electronic mail, and at certain times of the day the instructor would hold "office hours" through live audio- or videoconferencing. Fully interactive testing and review modules would be available: each correct answer would solicit a confirmation of the correct response, and each wrong answer would send the student back to the appropriate media and reference materials to gain a better understanding of the material. As Miller and Clouse (1993–1994) say,

> The various technologies available today such as broad-band broadcasts, microwave, electronic mail, videoconferencing, data base access, fiber optics, cable technology, full-motion video, and other related technologies will make it possible to communicate with large audiences at any moment in time at any near or distant location. [p. 193]

> New and further advancement in technology, especially in fiber optics and compressed video, will offer capabilities for interactive distance learning, both in education and business. Multimedia computer system interface with CD-ROM, video discs, databases, and future advances in computer technology will greatly change distanced learning programs. . . . Classrooms will no longer be defined as stationary nor a point in time. "Just in time learning" and "on-demand education" will be available through the combination of fiber optics, compressed video, interactive television and virtual learning environments. [p. 199]

References

Beatty, T. R., and Fissel, M. C. "Teaching With a Fiber-Optic Media Network: How Faculty Adapt to New Technology." *T.H.E. Journal*, 1993, *21* (3).

Douglas, S. G. "Digital Soup: The New ABCs of Distance Learning." *Educom Review*, 1993, *28* (4).

Miller, C. D., and Clouse, R. W. "Technology-Based Distance Learning: Present and Future Directions in Business and Education." *Educational Technology Systems*, 1993–1994, *22* (3).

Mizell, A. P., and Carl, D. R. "Inter-Institution Cooperation in Distance Learning." *T.H.E. Journal*, 1994, *21* (10).

Sphnepf, J., Masheyekahi, V., Reidl, J., and Du, D. "Closing the Gap in Distance Learning: Computer-Supportive, Participative, Media-Rich Education." *Educational Technology Review*, 1994, *3*.

Varma, I. "Reaching Out with Telecommunication." *Instructional Technology Systems,* 1993–1994, 22 (4).

Verduin, J. R., and Clark, T. A. *Distance Education: The Foundations of Effective Practice.* San Francisco: Jossey-Bass, 1991.

ROBERT D. STEWART *is academic network manager for Miramar College, La Mesa, California.*

A review of learning styles and their implications for distance learning.

Learning Styles: Implications for Distance Learning

Waynne Blue James, Daniel L. Gardner

Although distance learning may extend access to learning opportunities to adults who otherwise might not be served, options that merely replicate the problems and failures of conventional classrooms will not benefit students. The purpose of this chapter is to consider learning styles in the context of distance learning so the effectiveness of various options can be enhanced.

This chapter includes a review of learning styles and discusses a sampling of instruments available to assess individual learning-style differences. The second section provides a framework for viewing different types of distance learning. The third section explores suggestions on how to enhance distance learning by addressing individual learning styles.

What Are Learning Styles?

The definitions and terminology related to learning style are as varied as the individuals dealing with the concept. John Saxton's poem "The Six Blind Men and the Elephant" is an analogy that vividly illustrates this statement. In the poem, the six blind men chance upon different parts of the elephant; each man describes the part in relation to what he feels: a tree, a snake, a fan, a rope, etc. Researchers and scholars studying learning styles seem to have similar experiences: some consider physical modes of learning styles, some address cognitive issues, some consider the psychological or emotional aspects of learning styles, and others use a combination of some or all of these options. This leads to confusion and misunderstanding among those concerned with learning styles.

The ways individual learners react to the overall learning environment make up the individual's learning style. No universally accepted terminology exists to describe learning style and its various components; however, how people react to their learning environment is a core concept. Although the terms *learning style* and *cognitive style* are sometimes used interchangeably, the term *learning style* appears more regularly in print; it also appears to be the broader term. James and Blank (1993) defined learning style as the "complex manner in which, and conditions under which, learners most efficiently and most effectively perceive, process, store, and recall what they are attempting to learn" (p. 47). A model of learning styles as three distinct but interconnected dimensions provides a relatively simplistic format for addressing the myriad of possible options. These three dimensions include the perceptual (physiological or sensory) mode, the cognitive (mental or information processing) mode, and the affective (emotional or personality characteristics) mode.

Perceptual Dimension. Within the broad picture of learning styles, the perceptual dimension identifies the ways individuals assimilate information. It includes a biological response of the body to external stimuli. This may include input through physiological factors such as speech, movement, and any of the five senses. The perceptual dimension depends on the physical attributes of an individual's body to integrate information into the person's brain. It is the means through which information is extracted from the environment. Subsequent processing of the information is the purview of the cognitive dimension.

Various theorists/researchers have identified anywhere from three (Keefe and others, 1989) to seven (Gilley and French, 1976) perceptual elements. French (1975a, 1975b) proposed the concept of seven perceptual elements that include visual (pictures, diagrams), print (written words), aural (hearing), interactive (talking), haptic (touch), kinesthetic (movement), and olfactory (smell and taste). First Gilley (1975), then Cherry (1981), under the auspices of French, developed instruments to assess individual perceptual modality elements. The result was an instrument named the Multi-Modal Paired Associates Learning Test—Revised (MMPALT II). Research associated with the administration of this instrument provides information on perceptual modality.

Cognitive Dimension. Cognitive processes include the storage and retrieval of information in the brain. Information-processing habits represent the learner's typical ways of perceiving, thinking, problem solving, and remembering. Each learner has preferred avenues of perception, organization, and retention that are distinctive and consistent.

Flannery (1993b) proposed that cognitive information processing is discussed by experts in separate disciplines using terms such as *global* and *analytical* in cognitive psychology, *right* and *left brain* in hemisphericity (Herrmann, 1990), and *field-dependent* and *field-independent* in field articulation (Oltman, Raskin, and Witkin, 1971). Regardless of the terms used, *global, holistic, right-brained,* and *field-dependent* describe similar characteristics, whereas *analytical, focused, left-brained,* and *field-independent* can be used interchangeably as opposite ends of the same continuum (Ehrman, 1990). The first group of people prefers a broad overview of the subject, whereas the latter group seeks a detailed outline. Descriptors of the analytical style include step-by-step, sequential, inductive, abstract, and objective processes. People using the global approach favor simultaneous, deductive or intuitive, concrete, and subjective processes. Cognitive processes are not dependent on perceptual modalities.

Numerous learning-style inventories are available in this dimension. Some merely produce a bipolar scoring (McCarthy, 1986); others derive information on as many as thirteen separate subscales (Sternberg and Wagner, 1991). A few of the instruments currently available have undergone very thorough validity testing; for example, the Herrmann Brain Dominance Inventory (Herrmann, 1990) and Schmeck's Inventory of Learning Processes (Schmeck, Geisler-Brenstein, and Cercy, 1991) are two instruments validated by research studies. Many instruments in common use appertain to the cognitive dimension. Better known instruments include Kolb's Learning Style Inventory (Kolb, 1985), Gregorc's Style Delineator (Gregorc, 1982); Grasha–Riechmann's Student Learning Style Scales (Hruska, Riechmann, and Grasha, 1982), and the Hemispheric Mode Indicator (McCarthy, 1986).

Perhaps the easiest way to distinguish between the perceptual and cognitive dimensions of learning style is to draw an analogy with the computer. Perceptual modality equates to the information input to a computer system. Cognitive processing is similar to the tasks of the hard drive and memory. Input is essential to any subsequent manipulation of material: without input information, no processing of data can be accomplished. Both of these dimensions are fundamental to the operation of the computer, just as both dimensions are vital to the learning of an individual student.

The one dimension that the computer currently lacks is the affective component of learning. The affective dimension makes a human being distinct and unpredictable. It partially sets the human being apart from technology.

Affective Dimension. The affective dimension encompasses aspects of personality that relate to attention, emotion, and valuing. Affective learning styles are the learner's typical mode of arousing, directing, and sustaining behavior. Although affective learning-style components cannot be observed directly, they can be inferred from the learner's behavior and interaction with the environment. Ehrman (1990) believes that "psychological type affects the choice among the wide range of learning strategies available to an individual" (p. 15).

The social setting in which potential students prefer to learn is one component of the affective dimension; for example, whether students prefer to work with a partner, alone, or in a group is part of the affective dimension of learning styles. Ferro (1993) argues that "since the emotions are involved in every learning transaction, trainers and facilitators must attend to the affective domain" (pp. 32–33).

Instruments that directly address the affective dimension of learning include the Keirsey Temperament Sorter (Keirsey and Bates, 1984) and Honey and Mumford's Learning Styles Questionnaire (Honey and Mumford, 1989).

Numerous other instruments or inventories related to each of the three dimensions have been developed. Unfortunately, the results of reliability and validity testing are often inconclusive or contradictory.

Instrumentation

Careful selection of a learning-style instrument is crucial. Because of the pro-liferation of instruments, it is essential to objectively critique any instrument being considered. Selection of a particular learning-style instrument depends on several factors, the most important of which is the intended use of the data collected. Finding an available instrument and matching that instrument to its intended use is the next crucial step. Finally, selecting the most appropriate instrument to use is the last step in the process.

To determine whether an instrument is effective, we must consider the fol-lowing questions:

What concepts form the underlying considerations and design of the instrument? According to research, is the instrument valid and reliable?
What physical characteristics, administration difficulties, scoring and inter-
pretation issues, or costs affect the use of the instrument?

Many instrument developers have never addressed any of the concerns listed above. Typically, the instruments were developed because someone thought a learning-style inventory was a good idea. No formal measurement development procedures were applied to many of these instruments. There-fore, we should know whether the instrument selected accurately measures what it purports to measure or whether consistency occurs from one admin-istration to another. Because many educators tend to use available instruments, they naïvely consume the unlimited array of learning-style inventories.

For a more thorough discussion of these points, see James and Blank's arti-cle "Review and Critique of Available Learning Style Instruments for Adults" (1993).

James and Blank examined twenty different learning-style assessment instruments in relation to modality addressed, number of subscales, intended population, norms, validity, reliability, strength of research base, cost, and over-all instrument usability. Some of these instruments relate to one of the specific dimensions previously discussed; however, several instruments attempt to address all three dimensions at once. Dunn, Dunn, and Price (1988), Babich and Randol (1976), Hill (1977), and Keefe and others (1989) address the three dimensions of learning styles. Unfortunately, none have been validated by research; information on reliability is also weak.

One conclusion from the research accompanying James and Blank's article was that numerous research studies have failed to yield substantial evidence that the construct of learning style truly exists. With that as a caveat, however, some research does support prudent use of the concept of learning style. Hannum and Hansen (1989) concluded that "unfortunately the research evidence on learning styles is quite mixed. For all its intuitive appeal, it is rare to find clear examples of these styles that significantly influence the ability of a person to learn when his/her style is not attended to" (p. 119).

Because the evidence regarding the validity and reliability of many instruments is inconclusive and conflicting, it is imperative to use findings gathered from the instruments with great caution when decisions regarding students and programs must be made. Data derived from any instrument should be treated as potentially useful, but not critical information in the decision-making process.

Selection of a particular learning-style assessment instrument should be based on knowledge that the instrument is an attempt to obtain information to improve the learning effectiveness of individual learners. Learning-style instruments can be best used as an awareness tool that can enhance the technological constraints or benefits of a method used to deliver distance education.

Framework for Viewing Distance Learning

Moore (1990) defined distance learning as "all deliberate and planned learning that is directed or facilitated in a structured manner by an instructor . . . separated in space and/or in time from the learners" (p. 346). Garrison's (1989) model of three generations of distance learning (ranging from initial correspondence courses to audio-teleconferencing to more advanced computer-based options) can be used to examine the relation between the type of distance learning and learning styles.

An adaptation of Garrison's model presents four generations, which can be discussed in terms of the delivery system (such as mail or computers), the communication channels or modalities involved, method (group or individual), and interactive capacities (Billings, 1991). Generation One encompasses basic correspondence study including not only print materials, but also other mailable materials, including audio- and videocassettes. Audio and video teleconferencing are included in the second generation, whereas Generation Three relates primarily to computer technology capabilities. Generation Four includes some technological techniques that are not yet commonly used and more sophisticated options for the future (such as virtual reality or video desktop).

Generation One. Correspondence study primarily relies on the perceptual modality of print. Because print-oriented learning is one of the least effective perceptual modalities (James and Blank, 1991), instruction using only print media is not as beneficial as a mixture of modes. A recent research study concluded that students perform better and are happier with group interaction opportunities (Gunawardena and Boverie, 1992). Because correspondence study is a self-paced program, there is some concern over the effectiveness of this approach (Moore, 1990). In the cognitive dimension, correspondence study does not structure immediate and sufficient feedback.

Generation Two. Audio and video teleconferencing is another generation of distance learning. One example includes a system currently used in Oklahoma called talk-back television. Students gather in receiving locations with a video monitor and a telephone and can respond to the instructor in the sending studio. The instructor can talk to, but not see, the students at the receiving stations. Satellite teleconferences are a more sophisticated version of talk-back television.

Another Oklahoma system associated primarily with health care institutions is the telelecture system. This audio broadcast consists of telephone lines directed to any receiving station. Printed materials are usually provided before the air date. Barron and Orwig (1995) suggest that the greatest weakness of audio-only teleconferencing is the failure to add visual information.

A similar telelecture system is used in Hong Kong to deliver classes to participants on nearby islands. The instructor uses a specially designed booth to talk to students on twenty-four different telephone lines dispersed around the islands. The instructor can speak to each student individually if necessary. Again, printed materials are customarily distributed before broadcast.

Generation Two offerings generally provide an additional perceptual modality for students and feedback can be more immediate than with correspondence study.

Generation Three. Although Generation Three shares some characteristics with Generation One (individualized, self-paced learning), computers represent a much more sophisticated technology. Reliance on computers to teach rote memory information or discrete bits of information may not be the best use of a complicated technology. Research related to achievement and attitudes in computer courses indicates impact on all three learning-style dimensions.

Troutman and Kiser (1994) discuss the Learn from a Distance Program at the University of South Florida, which provides an alternative format intended to expand the effective delivery of instructional technology courses. Although they acknowledge that interaction is provided by large-group and optional small-group sessions, they allow no extra time to complete course work for students who cannot finish within the semester time frame.

A panel of experts recently judged computer activities to consist primarily of print and visual modalities (McCurry, 1995). Although visual is one of the three dominant perceptual modalities, print is not. Instructors who offer additional strategies such as group interaction activities can reach a wider range of student's learning styles.

According to research by Gunawardena and Boverie (1992), the delivery of instruction by various strategies does not affect how students interact with the media and methods of instruction but does affect student satisfaction. The authors report that their study was relatively small and caution that the results cannot be generalized; however, the research does lend some credence to the impact of affective factors when distance learning strategies are used.

Generation Four. The future of this generation is unlimited. As possibilities such as virtual reality or video desktop (two-way audio and video) become common, many problems associated with previous generations should become moot. Because these options are not yet in wide use, no research data are currently available; only speculation based on past experience is possible. The effectiveness of what works is "particularly important to remember in light of the diversity of experience and learning styles adults bring to the learning environment" (Stouch, 1993, p. 62).

As Florini (1990) wrote, "the mere use of technology to deliver instruction does not imply that the instruction is high in quality" (p. 383). In a similar vein, to acknowledge learning style differences without specifically addressing those differences will not help learners glean the most information from a particular learning experience.

Suggestions for Effective Use of Distance Learning

Although the literature presents a challenge to managers, designers, and instructors to address the various learning styles of adults participating in distance learning, few specific solutions are provided. Part of the difficulty lies not only in the range of technologies used, but also in the emerging nature of distance learning, which limits timely and relevant solutions. This section offers suggestions for the design and delivery of distance learning for adults by addressing instructional design principles and the importance of those principles to distance learning. Finally, learning-style variations based on the perceptual, affective, and cognitive modalities are related to the various generations of distance learning.

Instruction Design. Because the quality of instructional design is a crucial part of effective instruction, Florini (1990) asserts that "whether intended for electronic delivery or for more traditional means, efficient and effective instruction depends on good instructional design. Well-designed instruction intended for electronic delivery takes advantage of the strengths of a particular technology and compensates for its weaknesses. No amount of planning nor any particular technology can compensate for poorly designed instruction" (p. 384).

Gagne, Briggs, and Wager (1992) claim that because instructional design supports and extends learning by individual students, instruction must be systematically designed and based on knowledge of how human beings learn. Instructional design results in "a deliberately arranged set of external events designed to support internal learning processes" (p. 11). Dwyer (1990) noted that distance learning designers should be concerned with the same issues that designers of conventional instruction need to consider: "the psychological mechanisms through which the learner perceives, assimilates, interprets, stores and retrieves information" (p. 221).

Dick and Carey (1990) explain that traditional instruction typically involves teachers, students, and textbooks. The text contains information that is to be mastered; teachers are responsible for teaching that material to students. Teaching is generally interpreted as pouring the content from the book into the heads of the students so they can repeat the information on a test. Dick and Carey believe that "a more contemporary view of instruction is that it is a systematic process in which every component (i.e., teacher, students, materials, and learning environment) is crucial to successful learning" (p. 2).

156, 113

Dick and Carey (1990) provide a sequential model for the systematic development of instruction. They define nine basic steps:

1. Identify the instructional goal.
2. Conduct an instructional analysis.
3. Identify entry behaviors and characteristics.
4. Write performance objectives.
5. Develop criterion-referenced test items.
6. Develop an instructional strategy.
7. Develop or select instructional materials.
8. Design and conduct the formative evaluation.
9. Revise instruction.

Verduin and Clark (1991), in their discussion of distance education, state that "an instruction delivery system must be designed to help adult learners gain new behaviors. The term *instruction* in this case means the planning for and delivering of learning experiences for adults. It involves planning, teaching, interacting, learning, and assessment" (p. 155).

Verduin and Clark (1991) also recommend that the instructional design and delivery process for distance education proceed through five phases:

1. Assess entering behavior.
2. Specify behavioral objectives.
3. Specify learning unit and procedures.
4. Present learning unit and tasks.
5. Assess student performance. [p. 157]

Some of the steps or phases for Dick and Carey (1990) and Verduin and Clark (1991) are the same; however, Verduin and Clark's model addresses delivery, whereas Dick and Carey's model concentrates on development.

Instruction Design and Distance Education. Moore (1990) recognizes the critical nature of design activities in support of correspondence study as a form of distance learning. He notes that in all teaching there are two phases. The initial phase occurs without the learner, before instruction begins; the final phase occurs with the learner and supports instruction. Moore identifies these two phases, originally proposed by Jackson, as preactive and interactive. Preactive activities are accomplished apart from the learner. The teacher, leader, or designer prepares objectives, selects instructional strategies, and prepares materials. Moore observed that "while preactive teaching is deliberative, a highly rational process, interactive teaching is more spontaneous and to some extent controlled by the students' questions, requests, and reactions" (p. 348). He believes that the dichotomy between the two types of activities helps designers understand the salient features of distance learning. He describes the distance learning process as being more rational than emotional and more controlled and thorough than conventional education. It is private and typically between two individuals rather than public, in large face-to-face groups, as classroom teaching often is. In Moore's discussion of distance education, he states that although distance learning does not offer physical closeness, it does have the potential to offer closer psychological proximity than large, auditorium-type classes.

In distance learning, the preactive, program design stage is especially crucial. The designer must plan for large numbers of learners without knowing who they are, instruction can occur over longer time periods than classroom instruction, and because materials may be used for four or more years, they require careful structuring to assist a potentially large and diverse learner population. These possibilities demand that there be greater investment in course design beforehand.

Technology and Learning Styles. Distance learning programs require careful and deliberate instructional design steps. Ultimately, learning should be supported efficiently and effectively with technology that is appropriate for the learners and learning. Florini (1990) cautions that the nature of technology used for distance learning activities should be carefully considered as part of the design process. She believes that "using technology to enhance instruction means that some value is added to the instruction due to taking advantage of the characteristics of technology" (p. 383). In other words, using technology alone without considering individual differences articulated by learning styles is futile.

Granger (1990) suggests that distance education program designers can tailor the program to a student's needs in several ways:

Academically (content areas included)
Pedagogically (the combination of content and methods)
Experientially (studies that build on a student's background and incorporate experiential components)
Technologically (media used for various studies and modes of communication).

Verduin and Clark (1991) state that "those designing distance education should, moreover, pay attention to differences among adults—in individual learning styles, preferences for acquiring new knowledge and skills, and levels of maturity or ways of responding to new learning situations" (p. 32). Furthermore, they indicate that "each adult learner is different from other adult learners. Each adult possesses different beliefs, values, needs, attitudes, self-concept, and past experiences that must be considered as planning for the learning experience progresses . . . [and] to achieve the desired outcomes, individual considerations must be made" (p. 164). They also advocate that "learning styles complicate the distance educator's job, but . . . must be considered during early planning activities" (p. 29).

Dwyer (1990) feels that instructional quality and attention to learning styles cannot be left to chance. He states that instruction must be designed with learner differences in mind "so that [the activities] can be efficiently utilized by broad bands of learners possessing similar learner-related characteristics" (p. 222).

Design Enhancements and the Perceptual Mode. As stated earlier, within the broad picture of learning styles, the perceptual modality dimension identifies the ways people assimilate information for external sources. This section presents several strategies for consideration by the distance learning designer or facilitator in attending to differences in perceptual preferences among program clients. Strategies are organized according to those that are preactive and those that are interactive. Preactive actions occur before the implementation of the distance education course. Interactive actions occur during the delivery of the course.

In some ways, the perceptual modality is one of the easier dimensions to address because it is readily apparent whether the designers are meeting a variety of perceptual elements. For example, it is easy to add visual material (drawings, graphs, or pictures) to any printed materials. In methods that are primarily auditory, the incorporation of print and visual media can address the learning preferences of different students and enhance learning. Technically, it is possible to teach one unit in each of the seven perceptual modalities advanced by French; however, as a practical matter of time and creativity, this is often not possible. By providing as much variety as possible, the instructor can address different individual styles throughout the presentation. Research previously conducted (James and Blank, 1991) indicates that the three most commonly preferred modalities are visual, interactive, and haptic. Aural and print elements are not the primarily preferred elements. Because interactive is one of the top three elements, it is beneficial to provide opportunities for students to interact with other students in small-group discussion sessions or structure question-and-answer sessions. Perhaps infusing at least the three most dominant perceptual learning elements can offer improved learning means for students with those strengths. Print-based materials can always be supplied. The aural modality, although a basis for several of the generations, could be enhanced for activities that are print-based, such as correspondence study, by telephone conference sessions if students desire.

Design Enhancements and the Cognitive Mode. Cognitive processes include information-processing habits that represent the learners' typical ways of perceiving, thinking, problem solving, and remembering. Several strategies are available to the distance education designer in attending to differences in cognitive preferences among program clients. These relate to the structure of the program and the nature of materials and media.

Crafting the overall structure of the program offers designers the opportunity to consider the following options:

Providing for a diagnostic and prescriptive process to assign participants to programs
Designing programs to provide alternative tracks or instructional sequences depending on identified learner needs and preferences
Structuring content into small units

Providing for active participation of distance learners

Providing distance learners with an overall map or flowchart depicting the major components of the program

Designing and providing participants with a study guide that is easy to use

Ensuring that study guides are easy-to-use, informal, and direct and provide for practice and self-reflection

Structuring each unit with clear objectives.

Design Enhancements and the Affective Mode. The affective dimension encompasses aspects of personality related to attention, emotion, and valuing. Although affective learning-style components cannot be directly observed, they can be inferred from the behavior of the learner.

Several strategies are available to the distance education learning designer in attending to affective mode variation among program clients both before and during the implementation of the program:

Design a process to enable participants to become acquainted with the program facilitator or instructor, as well as with each other.

Provide for personalized communications with each participant before implementation or during initial program segments.

Design options to provide distance learners with choices about content and process.

Use an empathic and informal style in written and spoken components of the program.

Provide images and language that include different cultural perspectives.

Design and use a process for peer support among distance learners.

Communicate with distance learners as if they were in the near proximity.

Communicate with students by name.

Establish and maintain a regular and active dialogue with and among distance learners.

Use low-threat testing processes if testing is essential.

Summary

Distance learning provides a needed alternative for many adult students, but attention to individual differences, as currently practiced, is less than desirable. Concern for all of the factors involved with learning styles related to instructional design would undoubtedly improve the learning effectiveness of various distance learning offerings, but attention to some basic aspects of adult education should not be forgotten. As new technologies become commonplace, respect for individual differences and knowledge of learning-style idiosyncracies will undoubtedly improve learning effectiveness if these ideas are incorporated into the instructional design of distance learning.

References

Babich, A. M., and Randol, P. "Learning Styles Inventory Reliability Report." Unpublished manuscript, Wichita Public Schools, Kans., 1976.

Barron, A. E., and Orwig, G. W. *Multimedia Technologies for Training.* Englewood, Colo.: Libraries Unlimited, 1995.

Billings, D. *Distance Education Symposium: Selected Papers, Part 2.* Papers presented at the American Symposium on Research in Distance Education, University Park, Penn., May 1991. ACSDA Research Monograph number 8. (ED 371 750)

Cherry, C. E., Jr. "The Measurement of Adult Learning Styles: Perceptual Modality." Unpublished doctoral dissertation, Department of Curriculum and Instruction, University of Tennessee, 1981. (*Dissertation Abstracts International* 42, 09A)

Dick, W., and Carey, L. *The Systematic Design of Instruction.* New York: HarperCollins, 1990.

Dunn, R., Dunn, M. K., and Price, G. E. *Productivity Environmental Preference Survey.* Lawrence, Kans.: Price Systems, 1988.

Dwyer, F. M. "Enhancing the Effectiveness of Distance Education: A Proposed Research Agenda." In M. G. Moore, *Contemporary Issues in American Distance Education.* New York: Pergamon Press, 1990.

Ehrman, M. "Psychological Factors and Distance Education." *American Journal of Distance Education,* 1990, 4 (1), 10–24.

Ferro, T. R. "The Influence of Affective Processing in Education and Training." In D. D. Flannery (ed.), *Applying Cognitive Learning Theory to Adult Learning.* New Directions for Adult and Continuing Education, no. 59. San Francisco: Jossey-Bass, 1993.

Flannery, D. D. "Global and Analytical Ways of Processing Information." In D. D. Flannery (ed.), *Applying Cognitive Learning Theory to Adult Learning.* New Directions for Adult and Continuing Education, no. 59. San Francisco: Jossey-Bass, 1993.

Florini, B. M. "Communications Technology in Adult Education." In M. W. Galbraith (ed.), *Adult Learning Methods.* Malabar, Fla.: Krieger, 1990.

French, R. L. "Teaching Strategies and Learning." Unpublished manuscript, Department of Curriculum and Instruction, University of Tennessee, 1975a.

French, R. L. "Teaching Style and Instructional Strategy." Unpublished manuscript, Department of Curriculum and Instruction, University of Tennessee, 1975b.

Gagne, R. M., Briggs, L. J., and Wager, W. W. *Principles of Instructional Design* (4th ed.). New York: Harcourt Brace Jovanovich, 1992.

Garrison, D. R. "Distance Education." In S. B. Merriam and P. M. Cunningham (eds.), *Handbook of Adult and Continuing Education.* San Francisco: Jossey-Bass, 1989.

Gilley, D. V. "Personal Learning Styles: Exploring the Individual's Sensory Input Processes." Unpublished doctoral dissertation, Department of Curriculum and Instruction, University of Tennessee, 1975. (*Dissertation Abstracts International, 36,* 08A)

Gilley, D. V., and French, R. L. "Personal Learning Styles: Exploring the Individual's Sensory Input Processes." Paper presented at the annual meeting of the American Educational Research Association, San Francisco, Calif., 1976. (ED 124 504)

Granger, D. "Bridging Distances to the Individual Learner." In M. G. Moore (ed.), *Contemporary Issues in American Distance Education.* New York: Pergamon Press, 1990.

Gregorc, A. G. *An Adult's Guide to Style.* Maynard, Miss.: Gabriel Systems, 1982.

Gunawardena, C. N., and Boverie, P. E. *Impact of Learning Styles on Instructional Design for Distance Education.* Paper presented at the World Conference of the International Council of Distance Education, Bangkok, Thailand, November 8–13, 1992.

Hannum, W., and Hansen, C. *Instructional Systems Development in Large Organizations.* Englewood Cliffs, N.J.: Educational Technology Publications, 1989.

Herrmann, N. *The Creative Brain.* Lake Lure, N.C.: Brain Books, 1990.

Hill, J. E. *Cognitive Style Mapping.* Bloomfield Hills, Mich.: Oakland Community College, 1977.

Honey, P., and Mumford, A. *Learning Styles Questionnaire.* King of Prussia, Pa.: Organization Design and Development, 1989.

Hruska, S. Riechmann, S., and Grasha, A. F. "The Grasha–Riechmann Student Learning Style Scales." In J. W. Keefe (ed.), *Student Learning Styles and Brain Behavior*. Reston, Va.: National Association of Secondary School Principals, 1982.

James, W. B., and Blank, W. E. "A Comparison of Adults' Perceptual Learning Style and Their Educational Level." *Mountain Plains Adult Education Association Journal of Adult Education*, 1991, *19* (2), 11–21.

James, W. B., and Blank, W. E. "Review and Critique of Available Learning Style Instruments for Adults." In D. D. Flannery (ed.), *Applying Cognitive Learning Theory to Adult Learning*. New Directions for Adult and Continuing Education, no. 59. San Francisco: Jossey-Bass, 1993.

Keefe, J. W., Monk, J. S., Letteri, C. A., Languis, M., and Dunn, R. *Learning Style Profile*. Reston, Va.: National Association of Secondary School Principals, 1989.

Keirsey, D., and Bates, M. *Please Understand Me: Character and Temperament Types*. Delmar, Calif.: Prometheus Nemesis Books, 1984.

Kolb, D. A. *Learning Style Inventory*. Boston: McBer, 1985.

McCarthy, B. *Hemispheric Mode Indicator: Right and Left Brain Approaches to Learning*. Barrington, Ill.: Excel, 1986.

McCurry, P. "A Developmental Study of Effective Instructional Activities for Perceptual Modality Dominance in Tennessee Marketing Education." Unpublished doctoral dissertation, College of Education, University of Tennessee, 1995.

Moore, M. G. "Correspondence Study." In M. W. Galbraith (ed.), *Adult Learning Methods*. Malabar, Fla.: Krieger, 1990.

Oltman, P. K., Raskin, E., and Witkin, H. A. *Group Embedded Figures Test*. Palo Alto, Calif.: Consulting Psychologists Press, 1971.

Schmeck, R. R., Geisler-Brenstein, and Cercy, S. P. "Self-Concept and Learning: The Revised Inventory of Learning Processes." *Educational Psychology*, 1991, *11* (3–4), 343–362.

Sternberg, R. J., and Wagner, R. K. *MSG Thinking Styles Inventory*. Tallahassee, Fla.: Star Mountain Projects, 1991.

Stouch, C. A. "What Instructors Need to Know About Learning How to Learn." In D. D. Flannery (ed.), *Applying Cognitive Learning Theory to Adult Learning*. New Directions for Adult and Continuing Education, no. 59. San Francisco: Jossey-Bass, 1993.

Troutman, A., and Kiser, L. *Diversifying Instructional Delivery: Design and Implementation of a Distance Learning Program Using Telecommunications*. Paper presented at the meeting of the Society for Technology and Teacher Education, Washington, D.C., March 1994.

Verduin, J. R., Jr., and Clark, T. A. *Distance Education: The Foundations of Effective Practice*. San Francisco, Calif.: Jossey-Bass, 1991.

WAYNNE BLUE JAMES is professor of adult and vocational education, University of South Florida.

DANIEL L. GARDNER is assistant professor of adult and vocational education, University of South Florida.

This chapter offers techniques for creating a learning community in cyberspace.

Community and Computer-Generated Distance Learning Environments

Dale L. Cook

One of the continuing topics on the agendas of institutions and organizations today is the concept of community or, more accurately perhaps, the need to develop or find a sense of community. At Kent State University, for example, developing a sense of community is included in the institution's strategic plan and is one of ten goals of its president for the 1994–1995 academic year. Some fear what they believe is the inevitable further deterioration of whatever is left of community, and lay blame to advances in technology (Postman, 1985; Keyes, 1975). This chapter is written to initiate a more frank discussion of the impact of technology in human terms, for people as individual learners and as members of learning communities, and to discuss implications for learning facilitators. We begin with a brief discussion of community and what this term has come to mean.

Community

For many people, community is the place where they live: their neighborhood and where their kids go to school. However, for an increasing number of people, community has little to do with where they live. In *The Community of the Future and the Future of Community*, Morgan (1957) described the future community as one where geography was not a prerequisite. According to Morgan, a core of shared common interests and values forms the basis for community, within or outside of geographic space. Recalling Cantelon's statement in Chapter One regarding how distance education transcends time and space, it is important to realize that although time is required to adjust

NEW DIRECTIONS FOR ADULT AND CONTINUING EDUCATION, no. 67, Fall 1995 © Jossey-Bass Publishers

to an understanding of community not singularly rooted in geography, many would agree that such a change is occurring in our society (Dyson, Gilder, Keyworth, and Toffler, 1994). It is not that community cannot, or does not, exist in neighborhoods or cities, but simply that community is not limited to physical space. Think about it for a moment. Where do you find community? Do you have closer relationships and identify more with people you work with, or the people you live next door to? Has your community, and the way you define it, changed over the years?

Indeed, we find community in different places and through different means; in fact, many of us belong to multiple communities. Increased numbers of computer-literate people are getting on-line and connecting with people with whom they share common interests and values (whatever they may be). The extent to which these people are learning or experiencing community is an interesting point of discussion.

The cover page of an article written by Ralph Keyes (1975) illustrates the continuing concern, and even fear, that he and others have about the negative impact of technology on community. Four human figures seemingly made of concrete are depicted on the cover page; not one of the figures is looking at or able to communicate with the others. Keyes makes the point that as humans we crave community, but often make choices based on needs such as convenience, mobility, and privacy that lead us away from finding it. For example, we like the feeling of community we find at the now increasingly rare corner grocery store or hometown bank, but we often choose to shop at the lower priced megalopolis "everything you could ever want" grocery and the out-of-state bank with the highest savings rate of interest. We sometimes hear others complain about a loss of community, or feeling of belonging, but according to Keyes, "we didn't lose community. We bought it off."

If we did buy off community, one may argue that technology (from Gutenberg and the printing press to the industrialization of the automobile and mass transit to television) has been used as currency. For many years, computer technology has been feared as a destructive force. More and more people voice concern about getting lost in cyberspace, the information explosion, and about becoming computer widows and widowers.

Although technologies are often touted as neutral tools, some are criticized as more negative than others. Television, for example, is often cited as having a negative impact on society due to a variety of factors, not the least of which is the lack of opportunity for active participation (Postman, 1985). Such lack of active participation and activity led to the 1970s characterizations of people as couch potatoes. Growing numbers of people living as passive media recipients, due in part to television, is cause for concern in our society. In the long term, choices made in favor of a passive-recipient life may lead to lower levels of social responsibility and, according to James (1967), perhaps disintegration of the individual, the community, and ultimately even society as we know it.

Community Connections in Cyberspace

There are many examples of how those who bounce along on the cyberspace autobahn find community. A few sites are presented here to briefly illustrate this mode of travel for the benefit of readers who have not yet experienced it. The reader is also referred to Chapters Five and Six in this issue for examples of distance education communities that exist at the undergraduate and graduate levels. Those who use e-mail but have not ventured beyond it should think about what they used to say about e-mail, and how difficult they thought it was going to be to get started. Most people who now use e-mail would not voluntarily give it up, but for many, it was not long ago that they were saying that they did not really want it or need it. In many ways, the same can be said for the post-mail features of cyberspace.

The Whole Earth 'Lectronic Link (WELL) is an on-line service that provides access to people and ideas, and according to its worldwide web home page (an "address" or "place" on the web), is considered by many to be the birthplace of citizen-based virtual community. The service provides more than 200 conferences, each with "a distinct sense of place . . . like a neighborhood pub, a seminar, a dinner table or a town meeting." (To learn more about WELL, use the Universal Resource Locator, or URL. Its electronic address is www.well.com/about.html.) Similar services are offered on other proprietary on-line services providers (such as America Online, Prodigy, and CompuServe) and on various locations on the Internet, including news groups.

The Internet is free to those with access. Continual reductions in access fees are making the Internet more readily available to more and more people. The Center for Astrophysics at Harvard University has a web page titled Soc and Rec Club. The club's home page identifies the purpose of the club: "The Soc and Rec Club exists to help develop a sense of community at the CFA" (URL www.harvard.edu/src/homepage.html).

The Sociable Web (URL persona.www.media.mit.edu/socialWeb/) is a project that uses a modified web browser and server. When it is used on web pages served by a social web server, it shows who is on the web page and it allows the user to strike up conversations with them. People can be shown with their names and host machine, or by a small graphic.

SANDS (URL www.vicnet.net.au/vicnet/community/sands.htm) is another web location. The purpose of SANDS is to provide a support group for parents who have experienced a miscarriage, stillbirth, or neonatal death. It is not intended as primary treatment for parents with grief problems. However, it does provide support as an adjunct to therapy, both on-line and through a network of local contact groups.

The above illustrations represent examples of how people are beginning to find community in cyberspace. The more experience gained in cyberspace connections, the easier it is to understand and agree with Dyson, Gilder, Keyworth, and Toffler (1994) when they intimate that it is clear that cyberspace will play an important role in bringing together the diverse communities of tomorrow and in facilitating the creation of "electronic neighborhoods" bound together not by geography but by shared interests.

Community in the Classroom

Many have suggested that students learn best in an environment where a sense of community exists (Freire, 1973; Fingeret and Jurmo, 1989; and Shor, 1992). Coleman (1982) attributes some portion of the success experienced in private, especially church-related schools to the sense of belonging and community that exists there. Detractors of the use of computer-mediated distance learning cite the inability of computer-generated environments to duplicate the community of the traditional classroom as a major argument. Although computer-generated learning environments cannot currently duplicate the community of the classroom, two considerations should be noted.

First, we do not know how often community actually develops in classrooms. The assumption that a sense of community exists among students in traditional classrooms may be false in many or even most classrooms. Indeed, the development of community in classroom instruction may more likely be a romantic interpretation of the one-room schoolhouse. Second, yesterday's computer-assisted instruction is changing. Visual and audio together with evolving virtual reality technologies are making classroom experiences of community more likely. By offering the ability to control learning context at the flip of a switch, virtual reality represents a powerful way to open new paths of learning that will require the attention of educators. Furthermore, most technological developments are not limited to multimedia software designed for classroom use. These tools are increasingly becoming available on the Internet, and as a result the classroom has expanded to include groups of students, experts, and learning facilities from around the world, all with an interest in giving and receiving information.

Advantages of Adult Learning in Distance Education

The existence of distance education learning opportunities in computer-mediated environments on the Internet (or through other on-line networks) will not guarantee the occurrence of learning or social construction of knowledge any more than the existence of classrooms. Both require people who actively participate in life, seeking experiences to grow and learn. These are the people who will look for others who share their values and interests, and who will find communities in cyberspace, whether in nonformal, avocational areas or other areas more organized or formal in structure. Adult educators have argued for years that learners need to be more active participants in their learning (Brookfield, 1985; Knowles, 1975). People who assume responsibility for learning actively participate in life, and tend to view new experiences as opportunities for growth. The reflection of experience in relation to knowledge gained in previous experience is how we learn, and in learning that we grow (Lindeman, 1990; James, 1967; Knowles, 1975; Horton and Freire, 1990). Without a willingness to participate, reflect, and learn, opportunities for new potential experiences diminish and we are destined to experience what we already know. James (1967) would call this condition relation starvation. If our purpose in life is to become all we can, learning is indeed lifelong and we are always in the process of becoming. Again, Lindeman (1961) and James (1967) would say that to the extent people discontinue their attempts to experience, learn, and grow, the opposite occurs.

The growth of resources available on the Internet will help develop self-directed learners. This will occur simply because the Internet offers something for everyone (no matter what their interest may be) and because it is an effective and efficient way for people to connect with others who share mutual interests. As a result, many who have disassociated and have become passive recipients of life are afforded increased opportunities to become active participants. Adult educators have an important role in assisting increased numbers of people who want to become effective self-directed learners.

The older adult population's increasing use of cyberspace illustrates the point of active participation. Many older adults who had become disconnected or alienated from society are turning to Senior Net (a proprietary on-line service for seniors) and the Internet. In addition to news groups for seniors on the Internet, two cities have web pages: Boulder, Colorado (bcn.boulder.co.us/community/senior-citizens/center.html) and Blacksburg, Virginia (www.bev.net:80/community/seniors/). Older adults are learning and connecting with people around the world. They are also finding that their experiences matter, that people are interested in the knowledge gained through their life experience. Other groups of people are having similar experiences, largely because the Internet does not discriminate by gender, race, color, or ability level. As strange as it may seem, some people have married people they met on-line, including the technology coordinator for a branch campus. He and his wife communicated on-line for two years before they met and were married.

Integrating the Development of Community in Distance Education

By their actions, some seem to believe that it is possible to mandate community. Of course, this is impossible. Community must be developed from the inside out, and cannot be mandated. Just as it is difficult for organization leaders to develop community in their organizations, so too is it for learning facilitators in computer-mediated learning environments. A line in the syllabus that points to the importance of community in the development of on-line learning experience will not automatically cause the student to do what is necessary to achieve it. There is nothing wrong with noting the importance of community building in the syllabus, but the facilitator must find ways to help the learner develop it.

We have discussed examples of how people use the Internet to develop associations with each other, and at times even a sense of community. It follows that the same can occur in organized learning activities provided through computer-mediated environments. Once facilitators decide it is important to develop community among their students, the question becomes how it can be done, especially in a computer-mediated distance learning environment. The following suggestions are offered as an attempt to help distance educators develop a sense of community among their students.

A common teaching strategy used in traditional on-site classrooms to create an environment where community building can occur is small-group instruction. However, small-group activity need not be limited to on-site instruction. Assignments can be given to small groups of students (five or six) in distance education as well. Given the students' absence of contact in physical space, it may be more important for them to communicate in small groups when learning in computer-mediated distance learning environments. One way a facilitator could initiate small-group activity is by asking a group to search cyberspace for information not directly related to course content to help the groups develop as teams. Internet hunts (or surfing) designed by the facilitator or created by students can be used for this purpose. Net experiences not directly associated with course content are less threatening, help students gain a comfort level with the medium, and establish mutual trust, respect, and a real sense of control and ownership.

Learning partners could be used as a means of helping inexperienced learners become comfortable with the medium. Student pairings on-line provide a means for students to discuss questions about assignments, as students in a classroom often do between breaks in classes.

Facilitators of computer-generated distance learning environments must be flexible and patient. These characteristics are needed in the instruction of adults regardless of setting, but perhaps they are more critical in a computer-generated environment where learning occurs over a distance. Students new to this medium will experience some degree of difficulty getting on-line, no matter how clear the directions may be. Differences in communication software, modems, and on-line connect service are all potential sources of problems for students. Additional difficulties surface later after initial connections are made including sending and receiving mail and files and navigating the Internet. Facilitators must be especially understanding, flexible, and patient when working with students who experience difficulty in these areas.

Students who learn through this medium also require more regular and consistent feedback, as they do not receive body-language feedback as classroom students typically do. Hence, frequent and regular feedback is more important in computer-mediated learning environments than in classroom learning. The facilitator should let students know that the student will receive information on a weekly basis, and if possible, on the same day each week.

Another strategy facilitators could use to help promote community among students is to develop a listserv for the course. A listserv is a software system used on the Internet that automates e-mail to enable asynchronous conferencing. Most e-mail software packages provide a way for users to create a mailing list, but a listserv allows the creation of a forum or discussion group. Facilitators and students can identify issues related to course content and discuss them on the listserv. Through these discussions, students have an opportunity to get to know and understand each other.

The purpose of this chapter has been to discuss community and its relationship to computer-mediated distance learning. Although it is understood that such a learning environment cannot duplicate face-to-face classroom instruction, it is also apparent that learning at a distance should not exclude the development of community. Facilitators of learning in these environments must recognize the importance of community development in instruction and use means to assist in its development.

References

Brookfield, S. *Self Directed Learning: From Theory to Practice.* New Directions for Adult and Continuing Education, no. 25. San Francisco: Jossey-Bass, 1985.

Coleman, J. *High School Achievement: Public, Catholic, and Private Schools Compared.* New York: Basic Books, 1982.

Dyson, E., Gilder, G., Keyworth, G., and Toffler, A. *Cyberspace and the American Dream: A Magna Carta for the Knowledge Age.* Paper on Internet; URL www.pff.prg/position.html, 1994.

Fingeret, A., and Jurmo, P. (eds.). *Participatory Literacy Education.* New Directions for Adult and Continuing Education, no. 42. San Francisco: Jossey-Bass, 1989.

Freire, P. *Education for Critical Consciousness.* New York: Seabury Press, 1973.

Horton, M., and Freire, P. *We Make the Road by Walking: Conversations on Education and Social Change.* Philadelphia: Temple University Press, 1990.

James, W. *The Writings of William James: A Comprehensive Edition.* New York: Random House, 1967.

Keyes, R. "In Search of Community." *National Elementary Principal,* 1975, 54 (3), 8–17.

Knowles, M. *Self-Directed Learning: A Guide for Learners and Teachers.* New York: Cambridge Books, 1975.

Lindeman, E. *The Meaning of Adult Education.* Montreal: Harvest House, 1961.

Lindeman, E. C. *The Meaning of Adult Education.* Norman: Oklahoma Research Center for Continuing Professional Higher Education, 1990.

Morgan, A. *The Community of the Future and the Future of Community.* Yellow Springs, Ohio: Community Service, 1957.

Postman, N. *Amusing Ourselves to Death: Public Discourse in the Age of Show Business.* New York: Viking Penguin, 1985.

Shor, I. *Empowering Education: Critical Thinking for Social Change.* Chicago: University of Chicago Press, 1992.

DALE L. COOK is associate professor of education at Kent State University, Kent, Ohio.

Distance education is a powerful force for changing the undergraduate curriculum.

The Undergraduate Curriculum and Distance Education

Gary E. Miller

Since the beginning of the technological revolution in the 1970s, distance education has taken on several distinctive forms that reflect the characteristics of different technologies and an ever-increasing mixture of technologies in individual distance education programs. One must understand the variety of practices in distance education in order to grasp the power of distance education as a change agent for the undergraduate curriculum, increasing its compatibility with the needs of adult learners.

The oldest form of distance education—independent study—assumes an individual student studying in isolation from other students and from his or her instructor. For many institutions, this form of distance education is a stable tradition of long standing; as a result, it is often overlooked in discussions of U.S. distance education, despite its contributions to increasing access to undergraduate programs. More recently, advances in telecommunications have permitted the development of a distributed classroom model of distance education that serves groups of students in a live, interactive environment. Currently, a third approach is evolving as a result of advances in computer-based communications, which allows for the creation of an asynchronous learning community. Each of these forms assumes a different set of relationships among students, faculty, and the subject matter being learned. This chapter looks at the impact of each of three kinds of distance education on undergraduate programs.

Independent Study and Undergraduate Education

The independent study model of distance education assumes that the educational experience has been structured to give students the greatest possible control over the time, place, and pace of education. These elements of learner-centeredness, which are also hallmarks of adult education, have become the classic definition of distance education. Within this very general definition, there are a wide variety of practices that can be grouped in three models. These models represent not so much differences in instructional purpose as they do differences in technology and in institutional purpose. However, the differences have proven to be significant in terms of how the practice of distance education has affected undergraduate education. They are correspondence study, telecourses, and the open university.

Correspondence Study Model. Correspondence study—which today is generally called independent study or independent learning—began in the United States in the 1890s in response to a very specific social dilemma: the need to improve the quality of life in rural farming communities and to improve the practice of agriculture at a time when many feared the loss of the nation's agricultural base due to the migration of people to cities during the industrial revolution. Initially, independent study was focused on noncredit instruction. Specifically, the goal was to train farmers in agriculture and related fields.

Correspondence study used the nineteenth-century counterpart to the national information infrastructure—rural free delivery—to reach newly empowered rural students. This correspondence required a reliance on the written word. Course guides gave faculty an opportunity to organize the scope and sequence of the courses in written lessons that replaced the normal lecture. Correspondence courses could integrate texts and printed visual materials. In turn, the students were required to respond in writing, through essays that demonstrated the student's reflective understanding of the material.

From its inception, correspondence study was seen by practitioners as a student-centered system. Penn State began a correspondence program in agriculture in 1892 (Pennsylvania State College, 1895). Two years later, the annual report of what was then called the Pennsylvania State College described the program as a home reading program modeled after the Chautauqua approach. The report also suggests that, from the beginning, distance education extended the boundaries of our universities; of the first four graduates of Penn State's program in agriculture, two were from Pennsylvania, one from Canada, and one from the Oklahoma Territories.

Over the years, correspondence study has evolved into a multimedia system at many institutions. Printed texts and course guides are complemented by other presentation media (such as audiocassettes, videocassettes, slide sets, and computer software), new forms of interaction (fax, phone conferences, electronic mail), and increased access to other learning resources (such as computer data bases and CD-ROM). The key to the model, however, remains with empowering the individual student to study independently and to control the time, place, and pace of study.

This approach, originally applied to noncredit instruction, eventually carried over into credit courses. Among the U.S. leaders in the use of independent learning for undergraduate programs are Penn State, Brigham Young University, University of Nebraska, and University of Wisconsin-Extension.

The economics of independent learning make it an excellent mechanism for delivering narrowly defined undergraduate degrees to widely scattered student populations. For example, Penn State offers associate degrees in dietetics, gerontology, and small business management.

For the most part, university-based correspondence programs are housed at state universities and land-grant institutions (the major exception is Brigham Young University) and operate as extensions of the university's residential curriculum. Often, these programs not only serve distant students but provide resident instruction students a second option for scheduling courses. As a result of this organizational structure, independent study has not been widely used to change the curriculum itself. Traditional colleges and universities have used independent study to extend their existing degree programs.

Telecourse Model. Whereas the independent study model was developed and is used primarily at larger state universities, the telecourse model is identified primarily with community colleges. As with correspondence study, the initial incentives in the development of this model were social and institutional rather than curricular. In the late 1960s and 1970s, many urban community colleges saw a dramatic increase in enrollments due to a combination of two factors: the growth of the baby-boom generation to college age and the development of open enrollment policies in some states as a way to increase access to college for poor and historically disadvantaged populations. This enrollment pressure occurred at a time when public television was in a period of rapid growth. Both community-owned stations and educational licensees saw service to education as a primary mission of what was then called educational broadcasting. As a result, several key community college districts began to experiment with the use of public television to reduce campus space pressures by delivering courses to students at home.

The basic telecourse model involves three elements: a text, a study guide, and a series of video lessons. A fourth component might be occasional on-campus meetings. Originally, the video lessons replaced the classroom lecture; as a result, the typical telecourse model consisted of thirty to forty-five half-hour video lessons. Over time, the video component of telecourses has moved away from the studio lecturer and is often a highly produced video documentary that explores a particular theme within a lesson, provides a case study, or illustrates the key elements of a lecture. The direct one-to-one correlations with the traditional number of classroom lectures has eroded, as telecourses have been developed to fit into public broadcasting schedules or have been developed around general audience series, such as *The Ascent of Man, Connections,* or *The Civil War.*

By the 1980s, the telecourse model had become a national trend in community colleges, as other community colleges and universities began to adopt for their own curricula telecourses produced by such pioneers in the field as Dallas Community College, Coast Community College, and Miami-Dade Community College. Local institutions would broadcast the video programs over local public television stations or cable access channels. Within states, colleges formed consortia to get the best prices for individual telecourses. In 1981, the Public Broadcasting Service (PBS) initiated an adult learning service that became a national broker for the distribution of telecourses. This centralized service greatly reduced the cost of telecourse licenses to individual colleges and universities and provided a national distribution outlet that helped stimulate external funding for telecourses. Since 1981, more than a million students have enrolled in courses offered by local colleges and universities using telecourse packages distributed by PBS (Watkins, 1991).

The telecourse model also has been advanced significantly by the Annenberg/Corporation for Public Broadcasting (CPB) Project. Since 1981, the Annenberg/CPB Project has funded the development and distribution of many highly used telecourse packages. The project raised the video production standards for telecourse production and helped bring this end of independent study into the mainstream of community college life and into many four-year curricula. Though designed for the at-home viewer, video programs from Annenberg/CPB telecourses have also been used to supplement and enhance on-campus undergraduate education.

More recently, the Annenberg/CPB Project has invested funds to help institutions develop institutional policies and procedures needed to create a more productive integration of telecourses in the undergraduate curriculum. These projects move beyond the production of materials to address issues of administrative and academic policy, faculty development, and student support services that are needed for an institution to fully incorporate distance education into a coherent extended-access curriculum.

Telecourses have had an important effect on the acceptance of distance education in the United States. The production of nationally delivered telecourses has added new dimensions to the treatment of subject matter in distance education. The Annenberg/CPB Project course on physics, for example, offered students highly visualized animations of physics concepts, as well as classroom lectures by internationally known physicists. In addition, telecourses developed as supplements to PBS series such as *Connections* and *The Civil War* bring major documentary materials into courses, greatly enriching the experience of isolated students.

Open University Model. The open university movement, which began with the establishment of the Open University of the United Kingdom in 1970, set out not only to increase access but to create a distinctive undergraduate curriculum. The Open University established the model of a free-standing distance education institution. Because its curriculum was designed entirely for students at a distance, it was able to use the course design process to create a unique, highly interdisciplinary curriculum and allowed students to earn complete degree programs at a distance.

The Open University model has been widely emulated around the world. In the United States, the concept was emulated in nontraditional institutions within state systems. The best examples of this approach are the University of Maryland University College and Empire State College in New York. Both programs began by adapting British Open University courses to the United States. Today, both maintain many of the characteristics of the British courses in their own course development activities. This includes a multidisciplinary approach and the use of a course team to develop materials.

Although few U.S. universities have fully adopted the open university model, it has had a broader impact thanks to the International University Consortium (IUC). Founded by the University of Maryland University College (UMUC) in 1980, IUC expands the open university model by making individual course packages available to its member institutions. IUC's original courses were UMUC adaptations of British Open University courses. More recently, it has developed its own courses, using the UMUC model. Courses such as *War and American Study, American Society, The Middle East,* and *Managing in Organizations* suggest the continued interdisciplinary approach taken by IUC.

Independent Study and Undergraduate Education. For more than a century, the independent study approach to distance education has served to extend the undergraduate curriculum to off-campus students. As noted by Cantelon in Chapter One, independent study, one of the oldest forms of distance education, has given learners more control over the time, place, and pace of study. Not incidentally, it has also had an impact on the resident instruction program of institutions that offer independent study. It is not unusual for resident instruction students to mix independent study courses with their regular on-campus courses. At the same time, it is not at all unusual for faculty who design materials for independent study to use them in their resident classes.

Telecourses have also brought new resources into undergraduate curricula. Video programs produced for nationally distributed telecourses are often used as in-class audio–visual support for resident courses.

However, with the exception of curricula that have emulated the open university model, independent study has not had a significant effect on the underlying assumptions and structure of the undergraduate curriculum. Its impact has primarily been to increase access to higher education (National University Continuing Education Association, 1994). In this respect, however, its impact has been significant, touching the lives of hundreds of thousands of students— many of whom are adults—in U.S. colleges and universities annually.

Distributed Classroom

The 1990s have seen the rapid growth of the distributed classroom model of distance education. As early as the 1950s, universities began distributing class sessions in popular courses on-campus by using closed-circuit television to connect small classrooms. The effect was to offset the lack of large lecture halls and to make better use of smaller facilities. The resulting one-way video, two-way audio method eventually took advantage of instructional television fixed service (ITFS) channels, state microwave networks, and ultimately satellites to extend the university's on-campus programs to branch campuses and selected worksites. Examples of off-campus distributed classroom systems have been in operation since the 1970s and include the Indiana Higher Education Telecommunications System, the satellite-based National Technological University, and numerous ITFS networks that connect individual colleges and universities with worksites (National University Continuing Education Association, 1995).

This model was greatly stimulated in the 1990s by the arrival of interactive compressed video telecommunications systems, to the extent that many people now define distance education in terms of interactive telecommunications. A recent legislative analysis report noted that every state currently has a distance education distributed classroom network of some sort in development.

The physical characteristics of the distributed classroom model define its educational approach. Whether the system uses microwave ITFS channels or dialup interactive video, as described by Stewart in Chapter Two, the systems share several essential characteristics. First, the distributed classroom is a real-time delivery system: it is live and, as a result, spontaneous. Second, the distributed classroom reaches fixed, predetermined sites chosen by the sponsoring institution rather than by the individual students; in this sense, the distributed classroom is defined more by its technological infrastructure than by any particular instructional design. Finally, the distributed classroom is marked by the opportunity for spontaneous, real-time interaction between instructor and learners.

Behind these characteristics are other assumptions that distinguish the distributed classroom from independent study. For example, the distributed classroom assumes that the institution retains control over the time and pace of study. Telecommunications is used to give students more options with regard to the place of study. Beyond that, this kind of distance education has more in common with traditional classroom study than with other kinds of distance education. Instruction can be highly spontaneous, highly interactive, even Socratic in nature, but the emphasis remains on the instructor-centered, lecture-based approach that characterizes most classroom instruction.

Although the distributed classroom model has been most attractive to graduate programs, the growth of statewide networks has also increased its use in undergraduate education, both for delivery of programs off campus and for sharing of resources among resident instruction programs at several campuses.

The Electronic University, a guidebook to telecommunications-based distance education programs, lists a wide variety of curricula that demonstrate the impact of this approach to distance education on undergraduate programs (National University Continuing Education Association, 1995). The guidebook profiles sixty U.S. colleges and universities that offer undergraduate courses via electronic distance education. The profiles demonstrate the broad range of undergraduate programs that are extended through electronic distance education. This includes individual courses to full degree in programs in curricula ranging from liberal studies to computer science. Perhaps the most common undergraduate degree program offered by these institutions is the bachelor of science in nursing. Many other undergraduate professional degrees are also represented, including fire protection administration, accounting, counseling psychology, paralegal studies, professional aeronautics, agriculture, electrical engineering, and health care administration. At the same time, this methodology is being used by some institutions to deliver more traditional academic programs such as liberal studies and Biblical studies.

The Electronic University also demonstrates that electronic distance education has evolved into a multimedia delivery system. For example, the New Jersey Institute of Technology offers a bachelor's degree in information systems through a combination of videocassettes and computer conferencing. Washington State University's bachelor's degree in social sciences uses a combination of cable television, computer conferencing, fax, public television, and satellite television. Rochester Institute of Technology offers a bachelor of science in applied arts and sciences that uses a combination of the technology described in Chapter Two: audiographics, cable television, computer conferencing, electronic bulletin boards, electronic mail, fax, public television, teleconferencing, telephone, and videocassette.

Interactive telecommunications has greatly expanded access to undergraduate education and has blurred the boundaries between continuing and resident instruction and, ultimately, between distance and classroom instruction. However, it has had little effect on the actual structure of the undergraduate curriculum.

Learning Community

Both independent study and the distributed classroom have had a significant effect on the access students have to undergraduate education; they have given students greater control over the time and place of study. They have also contributed, in varying degrees, to a more learner-centered approach to education, giving students greater control over the pace of study and making undergraduate education more attractive and accessible to adults. However, with the exception of the open university model, which has had relatively little impact in the United States, distance education has had little effect on the basic assumptions on which the undergraduate curriculum is based.

This situation is changing as newer technologies enter the distance education arena. The primary technological agents of change are computer-based communications, from e-mail to the worldwide web, and CD-ROM. These technologies, in combination with others already being used in distance education, offer students not only a much richer environment for spontaneous interaction, but greater control over the subject matter and over the pathways through that subject matter, creating a new kind of learning community.

The learning community approach to distance education assumes an instructional design in which the student uses a mixture of media. Each medium plays a specific part in articulating a complex learning environment.

These may include presentation media, such as print, videos and audiotape, and computer software; delivery media, such as broadcast/cable television, computer file servers, and CD-ROM; and interaction media, such as audio- and videoconferencing, electronic mail, keypad response systems, and digital voice response systems. In addition, students may have access to the range of library resources and data bases resident on the worldwide web.

Although the learning community approach calls on many media, it is defined less by the media themselves than by the learning environment that is created through the use of multiple media. The impact of learning technology is to greatly enrich the resources available to the student and thus increase the learner's control—and responsibility—in the overall process. The resulting learning environment is characterized by its focus on the learner and on enriching the resources available. Similarly, the use of multiple communications technologies creates an environment that is both asynchronous and spontaneous.

These key characteristics—asynchronous, resource-based, learner-centered, spontaneous—are responsive to the stresses that are currently reshaping the undergraduate curriculum. Access is no longer the primary driving force behind this type of distance education. The defining characteristic is no longer geographic distance, but learner control and an active learning environment that emphasizes learner interaction with resources, with other learners, and with the instructor.

In the process, the learning community approach is blurring the lines between distance education and resident instruction. As universities turn toward an undergraduate curriculum that is more collaborative, using resource-based instructional models on campus—including computer simulations, hypermedia-based studies, and the worldwide web and other on-line resources—the experiences of students on campus becomes less classroom-bound and more learner-centered. As a result, many adults are finding under-graduate education programs that are meeting their needs.

Conclusions

Distance education is moving with increasing speed into the mainstream of college and university life. At the undergraduate level, two primary approaches are emerging. One is a heightened individualized distance education model, based on the original correspondence model, that gives students greater flexibility and control over the learning environment. The second is the inheritor of the distributed classroom model, which provides for both group and individualized study, with the notion of a class section gradually being replaced by the idea of cohorts who work both collaboratively and independently in a resource-rich learning environment.

Although both of these models were designed originally to serve nontraditional students, the methods and media of distance education are taking their place on campus as our colleges and universities redefine the curriculum for an information age and attempt to serve a student population that is so diverse as to make outmoded the concept of a nontraditional student or delivery system. For the undergraduate curriculum, distance education is both a signal of change and a tool for change.

References

Pennsylvania State College. *Annual Report of the Pennsylvania State College for the Year 1894.* Clarence M. Busch, State Printer of Pennsylvania, 1895.

National University Continuing Education Association. *The Electronic Classroom: A Guide to Distance Learning Programs.* Princeton, N.J.: Peterson's Guides, 1995.

National University Continuing Education Association Division of Independent Study Research and Evaluation Committee. *Independent Study Profiles, 1992–1993.* Tuscaloosa: University of Alabama, 1994.

Watkins, B. L., and Wright, S. J. (eds.). *The Foundations of American Distance Education: A Century of Collegiate Correspondence Study.* Dubuque, Iowa: Kendall-Hunt, 1991.

GARY E. MILLER is assistant vice president for distance education at Pennsylvania State University.

Increasing numbers of adult learners complete graduate degrees through institutions that offer distance education options. Three examples of graduate distance education programs are described.

Graduate Degree Programs and Distance Education

Craig D. Swenson

Accelerating social, economic, demographic, and technological changes are forcing continuous reexamination of how we deliver education. Perhaps nowhere are the effects of change more evident than in graduate education; witness the rapid growth of graduate degrees offered via distance education. A catalyst to the growth and accessibility of graduate programs is the increased participation of nontraditional adult learners (Lynton and Elman, 1987). The ranks of adults seeking advanced degrees are growing for several reasons.

One reason relates to the information explosion and resulting advances in technology. These result, in turn, in ever-greater complexity in our social systems and institutions. According to Schön (1983), graduate and professional schools must shoulder the burden of preparing leaders in the disciplines and professions who deal with increasing complexity. With the recent emphasis on organizational learning, those who lead our institutions are becoming more aware of the need for members who can import knowledge—members who are continuously learning and who can teach others how to learn (Senge, 1991; Watkins and Marsick, 1993). Many organizations thus find it beneficial to encourage and fund the graduate study of seasoned employees who can apply the knowledge from their schooling to the organizational setting. These people serve as learning leaders in their organizations.

Another reason can be found in the transition to a new economy based on the use of knowledge and information. Corporate downsizing has hit the ranks of lower and middle management especially hard. Changes in the demographic composition of our work force have exacerbated the problem. Just as employees reach the career stage when they expect to move up, they instead find themselves displaced or their jobs threatened. To make themselves newly marketable, either as full-time employees or in the growing ranks of the contingency work force, these people often seek advanced degrees.

Other developing demographic and social phenomena may bolster this trend well into the future. Assuming predictions are correct, greater longevity will trigger a shift in society's perspective of age-related roles and behaviors. As this occurs, people will return to formal schooling more often as we adopt a cyclical rather than linear life-span perspective. Economic opportunity will be only one reason for seeking advanced schooling. For many others, personal growth and the fulfillment of life goals will drive their decisions to participate (Dychtwald, 1990; Gerber, Wolff, Klores, and Brown, 1989).

Finally, as noted in Chapter Two, technology has advanced to the point where high-quality education can be delivered to large yet dispersed populations at low cost. Populations once excluded by constraints of time, place, and pace now find advanced study accessible. Beyond the enhancement and expansion of educational access, computer-mediated communication offers exciting new avenues for effective new learning and research interactions (Dennis and Valacich, 1993; Harasim, 1987). Progress in information science is helping distance education emerge from its second-class status (Baird and Monson, 1992). Some state university systems now seek accreditation for their electronic education networks. In other states, existing institutions are posturing for control of distance education. So rapidly are things changing that a recent gathering of higher educators convened to explore how the traditional teaching and learning environments of colleges and universities are challenged, and even threatened, by on-line learning (DeLoughry, 1990).

Fit Between Distance Education and Graduate Education

The view that graduate education should differ from undergraduate education is widely shared. By the end of the nineteenth century, the North American university had adopted two very different educational models: the British model of undergraduate education, which emphasized teaching and learning, and the German model of graduate education, in which competency in research and scholarship was the goal (Anderson, 1993; Douglas, 1992; Pelikan, 1992). Based on this difference, graduate school is accepted as a place of more frequent and intense interaction between instructors and students. Debate and dialogue are expected to play a greater role among graduate students than among undergraduates, who are still learning the vocabulary of a subject (Queen's University, 1975). Teachers of graduate courses rate the development of higher-order thinking skills as a significantly more important instructional priority than do those who teach undergraduates (Swenson, 1995). Graduate students are also expected to exhibit real independence of effort and to perpetuate the image of the solitary scholar. Bowen and Rudenstine (1992) note that this creates an inherent and complicated tension between the need for intense contact between professors and graduate students and the seemingly contradictory need for solitary deliberation. Candy (1991, p. 185) calls the ideal relationship between student and advisor "assisted autodidaxy."

Creating distance education programs that are sensitive to these unique requirements of graduate study is a challenge to administrators and faculty members responsible for their design and implementation. In the remainder of this chapter, examples of three very different graduate degree programs that embody varied methods of distance education are discussed. This review is not intended to be comprehensive. The growth in programs of this type precludes a thorough inventory. Rather, these examples are intended as an overview of possible approaches to graduate distance education.

Examples of Graduate Distance Education Programs

There are numerous ways to classify distance education programs. For example, Verduin and Clark (1991) identify six categories based on commonly recurring education models. These range from institutions that offer degrees to students they have not directly taught, to traditional institutions that also offer distance options, to those created solely to teach students and grant degrees at a distance.

Another way to classify graduate distance education programs is by mode of delivery. As discussed in Chapter Two, these include independent or directed study; audio or video teleconferencing networks; on-line, computer-mediated conferencing; and clustered residencies. Developments in multi-media technology are blurring the lines between modes. Additionally, the modes do not represent discrete categories. Within each are ranges of delivery options. Video, for instance, can be one-way or interactive, live or recorded. Because modes can be mixed and matched within programs, classification has become increasingly difficult. New technologies and hybrid combinations present unique challenges to those charged with program assessment and accreditation (Garten and Hedegaard, 1993). For purposes of this chapter, three very different examples were selected to represent a wide range and combination of modes.

Virtual Campus: Walden University. For midcareer professionals, pursuing doctoral studies in the traditional university setting is difficult if not impossible. The cultures of most institutions foster the assumption that learners must participate in essentially the same doctoral experience as those in on-campus programs. Usually, this involves completion of coursework and doctoral seminars, and completion of one's original research, all while assuming regular teaching duties. For the younger graduate student whose goal is to continue on in an academic setting, this is a reasonable expectation. As the introduction to this chapter suggests, however, increasing numbers of working adults seek to complete doctoral degrees. In some cases, these people already teach at institutions other than where they do their doctoral studies. Many more do not intend to pursue traditional academic careers. Instead, they use their advanced degrees as internal consultants in their organizations, or to establish external consulting practices. For these students, most of whom do not have the luxury of quitting their jobs for two to three years while they complete their coursework, traditional programs are simply not a good fit.

In response, several institutions have been created whose missions are to serve the unique needs of these nontraditional doctoral students. Among the better known of these institutions are the Union Institute, Saybrook Institute, Nova Southeastern University, and Walden University. Walden was chosen for inclusion in this chapter because it represents an interesting mix of distance education delivery methods.

Headquartered in Minneapolis, Walden serves a student population made up of working adults who are most often midcareer professionals. Walden has been described as a dispersed residency distance education program. Learners participate in a mixture of centralized and clustered residencies, complete personalized learning contracts built around Walden's curriculum, join in voluntary on-line seminars, and perform independent original research. Thus, doctoral fellows are able to participate in a distance learning experience that satisfies the essential criteria of graduate study. With the exception of a three-week summer session, faculty and students rarely have face-to-face meetings.

At the program's outset, each student negotiates a comprehensive individual professional development plan (PDP) with a faculty advisor. The PDP is a vehicle to encourage critical reflection and also becomes a guide as the program of study progresses.

At the heart of Walden's program is its curricula: the seven knowledge area modules (KAMs). The KAMs provide the framework in which students are able to gain and demonstrate knowledge appropriate to the doctoral level.

For each KAM, using the university's structured curricula as a framework, each student develops a learning agreement with his or her faculty advisor or another KAM assessor. These agreements must be negotiated via telephone, fax, e-mail, or snail mail as both faculty and students are widely dispersed throughout the United States and abroad. Using the learning agreement as a guide, students gain knowledge by guided reading and writing under the tutelage of the faculty member.

At the appropriate time, students begin planning for their original research, which culminates in a doctoral dissertation. As in traditional doctoral programs, the student prepares a comprehensive dissertation proposal, which must be approved by his or her committee chair and defended before the other committee members. This occurs via a telephone conference call. Once the research is completed and accepted, the finished dissertation must also be presented via a telephone conference call to the full committee and the academic dean.

Through these activities, Walden fellows demonstrate that they are able to function independently as "solitary scholars." At the same time, Walden's program is also structured to a collegial environment considered essential for doctoral level education. This is accomplished in two ways.

The first is through attendance at periodic face-to-face residencies. At least once during their program—usually toward the beginning—Walden fellows are required to attend a month-long residency held each summer at Indiana University's campus in Bloomington. During this summer session, they listen to faculty papers, presentations, and responses; participate in small guided doctoral seminars; consult with faculty members; develop learning agreements; and use Indiana University's research library. Additionally, each student is required to attend one week-long residency during each academic year in which he or she is enrolled. These regional intensive sessions are held periodically at dispersed locations throughout the United States.

Another means by which interactive learning is fostered at Walden is through the use of e-mail and computer-mediated discussion groups on the Walden Information Network (WIN). The WIN also provides Walden's connection to the Internet. Through the WIN, students are able to participate in interactive seminars, workshops, and colloquia.

A common challenge faced by distance educators is providing access to research libraries and materials. This is especially crucial for graduate students, who are expected to complete original research. Walden has responded to this obstacle by establishing a long-term contractual relationship with the library at Indiana University. Walden maintains a full-time reference librarian and staff to serve the needs of learners at the summer sessions and throughout the year. Each student enjoys circulation privileges from the Indiana collection. The librarian is also available to perform electronic searches. Additionally, access to Indiana University's catalog is available through Walden's Internet Gopher server. This helps ensure that students are not restricted in their ability to access research materials.

A criticism of doctoral programs at many traditional institutions is that students often do not receive the level of support and mentorship they need to get through the rigors of study at this level. This is often cited as a primary reason why so many learners, who may have completed coursework and the comprehensive examination, fail to complete their doctoral research (Bowen and Rudenstine, 1992). If lack of support is a problem at traditional institutions, providing a strong support system is an even greater challenge to distance education institutions whose students are geographically dispersed. Learners who are strongly self-directed appear to stand a better chance of completing distance education programs. The good news for institutions that serve mid-career professionals is that older, mature enrollees are more likely than traditional students to have the strong motivation necessary to succeed at a distance (Holmberg, 1989).

On-Line Education: University of Phoenix. The University of Phoenix (UOP) Online Campus in San Francisco serves a distinctive adult student population using a teaching and learning model built around the needs of working adults. Like other UOP campuses, it attempts to incorporate the qualities of an interactive classroom-based learning environment. Unlike the other campuses, Online does so by electronically combining cohorts of students from many different locations who together complete master's degrees in business administration or organizational management. The locations and life situations of most Online students preclude them from attending classroom-based programs. Instead, learners use personal computers and modems as vehicles for communication. Computer-conferencing software defines the virtual classroom.

UOP's Online educational delivery system is called Apollo Learning Exchange, or Alex. (Apollo is the name of UOP's parent organization.) Menu screens and program application protocols emulate an electronic university, in some ways similar to a gopher server on the Internet. In the Online system, a student can get answers to administrative questions, talk to a counselor, download a university newsletter, participate in coffeehouse discussions, go to the library, or attend class.

Students, faculty, and staff can access Alex via most standard DOS or Macintosh communications programs. All communications are delivered in ASCII format, which allows participants to use a variety of word processors. They develop messages and files on their personal systems and upload to Alex. A standardized one-week, eight-hour orientation program acclimates new users to on-line education. Students learn to navigate Alex and learn standard protocol for communicating on-line. Its developers compare this orientation to taking new students on a "walking tour of the electronic university" (Lewis and Hedegaard, 1993, p. 70).

UOP's teaching and learning model for its classroom-based programs emphasizes a highly collaborative environment in which learners are active participants. Classes are small—they average fifteen students—and each student also participates in a smaller study group that meets outside of class to complete group assignments. Each graduate student is also required to complete a significant piece of original applied research directly related to his or her profession. The faculty is made up of practitioners who hold advanced degrees in their fields but work full-time. They are viewed by students more as peers and facilitators than as professors. This model seems also to fit the on-line environment well. There is one difference, however. Developers have discovered that optimum group size for computer-mediated groups seems to be slightly smaller—eight to twelve students rather than fifteen (Lewis and Hedegaard, 1993).

UOP Online makes use of asynchronous communication. Messages and files, representing homework and communication in the "classroom," are uploaded to Alex, where they are later downloaded by classmates and the instructor. Because of time constraints, synchronous or real-time computer-mediated communication appears to inhibit thorough and thoughtful responses when many participants are involved. The asynchronous mode fosters reflective, critical thought because it allows participants to think before they have to respond.

A standardized curriculum is used, with specific weekly deadlines for uploading homework and comments to classmates, study group members, and the instructor. This helps prevent students from getting lost in the open-ended potential of asynchronous communication. Lewis and Hedegaard (1993) report that a key to ensuring student success is to "establish clear deadlines for sub-mitting coursework and participating in classroom discussions. Otherwise, classroom communication loses a sense of closure from week to week" (p. 70).

These characteristics of UOP Online make it time- and place- independent. A student who travels can complete homework assignments and prepare dis-cussion responses on a laptop computer while flying on business, then upload work from a hotel room. Other students—shift workers, for instance—can schedule schoolwork at a time that accommodates their schedules rather than the institution's. In response to concerns that learners will not spend adequate time at schoolwork when they are not in the traditional classroom, Harasim (1987) found that on-line students actually spent significantly more time than do students in classroom courses. Students reported assuming greater individ-ual initiative for the course, as well as increased self-responsibility. They also agreed that while the instructor was involved, he or she did not emerge as the dominant voice in the on-line discussions and seminars.

Another distinctive characteristic of programs such as UOP's is that they facilitate many-to-many communication. Independent study is usually one-to-one. Until recently, distance education programs that include video used one-to-many communication (Harasim, 1987). In on-line education, any member is able to communicate with all other members of a group, network, or confer-ence. This creates an environment considerably different from that fostered by traditional pedagogy in higher education, where professors lecture and students have a more passive role. This characteristic introduces a democratic element into the electronic classroom that seems more consistent with accepted practice of adult education (Knowles, 1990; Brookfield, 1986). Lewis and Hedegaard (1993) note that having an equal chance to participate diminishes status as an inhibiting factor. They also suggest that it is more difficult for a student to hide in the typical on-line classroom. In a study that compared UOP Online students to UOP students in face-to-face groups, Hedegaard (1993) "found that students in computer-mediated groups manifested higher self-concept and esteem, placed a greater value on education to enhance their professional lives, and had a greater propensity toward risk-taking" (p. J4).

With all its advantages, UOP's Online program developers point out that text-based communication does have limitations. For example, UOP's program is limited in the use of media. Although technological advances are making multimedia applications via computer possible, these technologies require state-of-the-art hardware and firmware. The requirements for students to upgrade equipment and software may create a barrier to participation for many. One challenge is to accommodate both a mass market and emerging technology.

Performing graduate study via the on-line classroom is an interesting and promising new development in graduate distance education. It appears to sat-isfy the unique criteria of graduate study discussed earlier in this chapter. Still, this educational delivery system is still relatively young, and as Harasim (1987) notes, there are still many unanswered questions and almost endless possibil-ities for future research.

Space-Age Education: National Technological University. Educators have long accepted television as a valuable instructional medium. The effectiveness of television-based instruction is well established in the literature. In a review of more than 100 studies, Whittington (1987) found that learning outcomes of telecourse students were equal or superior to students in face-to-face courses. Verduin and Clark (1991) summarized findings of the limited collection of studies in which television is used at a distance in higher education rather than as an adjunct to conventional classroom teaching. They reported that "in all but one case, distance higher education via television yielded the same or better student achievement than conventional methods" (p. 92).

National Technological University (NTU) is unique among graduate-degree-granting institutions in that all instruction is provided through television. Located in Fort Collins, Colorado, NTU was created in 1984 to serve the advanced educational needs of engineers, scientists, and technical managers. NTU is a consortium of engineering schools from forty-six American universities and offers M.S. degrees in twelve engineering and scientific fields.

Through satellite networking, NTU delivers approximately 700 advanced technical courses to students at more than 600 sites throughout North America. These are regular classroom courses taught by professors at the participating institutions and broadcast live by satellite downlink to participating organizations, mostly large industrial or high-tech companies or government entities. Direct phone lines from these receiving sites to instructors' classrooms provide for student–faculty interaction. Students also have access to faculty members through e-mail, computer teleconferencing, and telephone office hours. They complete the same coursework as in-class students and send assignments in for grading.

According to Johnson (personal communication, February 1994), participating faculty members have become adept at tailoring coursework to meet the needs of both face-to-face and distance learners. They are able to integrate multimedia elements into their standard presentations to make instruction more visually stimulating. Creating a successful instructional environment is facilitated by the composition of the student body. The average age of students is thirty-three and, Johnson notes, they already hold bachelor's degrees in technical fields and are highly motivated. Participants give instructors above-average ratings and report that courses are challenging and directly applicable to their work environments.

The average NTU student completes required courses through professors at six to eight different universities—a fact that NTU sees as an advantage because it gives students a broad perspective of approaches to their discipline. Each course is transcripted and degrees are awarded by NTU. By the end of the 1995 school year, NTU will have awarded more than 800 degrees. They hold commencement via satellite in what Johnson (personal communication, February 1994) calls "the most complicated graduation ceremony on earth."

Conclusion

The programs described above furnish strong evidence that distance education programs can be designed to provide the rigor, collaborative environment, and assisted autodidaxy necessary for high-quality graduate-level study. Moreover, these examples illustrate that a wide range of delivery methods can be used to satisfy these criteria. Perhaps because they tend to serve nontraditional populations, or because they provide an experience dissimilar to that of most traditional academics, distance education programs continue to be viewed somewhat suspiciously. Also, the emergence of new communication technologies blurs geographical and institutional boundaries and threatens the sovereignty of states and regulatory agencies.

As these issues are settled, and as graduates of these programs demonstrate that they can contribute to their organizations and professions, graduate distance education programs will gain wider acceptance and support. It is also likely that emerging generations of scholars will not find new communication and information technologies as daunting. In the meantime, distance educators will do well to insist on high standards of academic quality and achievement and to demonstrate this quality through empirical research.

References

Anderson, C. W. *Prescribing the Life of the Mind: An Essay on the Purpose of the University, the Aims of Liberal Education, the Competence of Citizens, and the Cultivation of Practical Reason.* Madison: University of Wisconsin Press, 1993.

Baird, M. A., and Monson, M. "Distance Education: Meeting Diverse Learners' Needs in a Changing World." In M. J. Albright and D. L. Graf (eds.), *Teaching in the Information Age: The Role of Educational Technology.* New Directions for Teaching and Learning, no. 51. San Francisco: Jossey-Bass, 1992.

Bowen, W. G., and Rudenstine, N. L. *In Pursuit of the PhD.* New Haven: Yale University Press, 1992.

Brookfield, S. D. *Understanding and Facilitating Adult Learning: A Comprehensive Analysis of Principles and Effective Practices.* San Francisco: Jossey-Bass, 1986.

Candy, P. C. *Self Direction for Lifelong Learning: A Comprehensive Guide to Theory and Practice.* San Francisco: Jossey-Bass, 1991.

DeLoughry, T. J. "Will Higher Education Thrive or Wither in Cyberspace?" *Chronicle of Higher Education,* Jan. 13, 1990, p. A22.

Dennis, A. R., and Valacich, J. S. "Computer Brainstorms: More Heads Are Better Than One." *Journal of Applied Psychology,* 1993, 12 (4), 531–537.

Douglas, G. H. *Education Without Impact: How Our Universities Fail the Young.* New York: Birch Lane Press, 1992.

Dychtwald, K. *Age Wave: How the Most Important Trend Will Change Your Future.* New York: Bantam, 1990.

Garten, E. D., and Hedegaard, T. "The Rise of Computer Conferencing Courses and Online Education: Challenges for Accreditation and Assessment." Paper presented at the ninety-eighth annual meeting of the North Central Association of Colleges and Schools, Chicago, April 4–6, 1993.

Gerber, J., Wolff J., Klores, W., and Brown, G. *Life-Trends: Your Future for the Next 30 Years.* New York: Avon, 1989.

Harasim, L. "Teaching and Learning On-Line: Issues in Computer-Mediated Graduate Courses." *Canadian Journal for Educational Communication,* 1987, *16* (2), 117–135.

Hedegaard, T. "Learning Online and On Campus: A Comparison of Adult Students' Professional Attitudes and Values." *ED Journal,* 1993, *8* (8), J1–J6.

Holmberg, B. *Theory and Practice of Distance Education.* Boston: Routledge/Kegan Paul, 1989.

Knowles, M. L. *The Adult Learner: A Neglected Species* (4th ed.). Houston: Gulf Publishing, 1990.

Lewis, C., and Hedegaard, T. "Online Education: Issues and *Some* Answers." *Technological Horizons in Education Journal,* April 1993, pp. 68–71.

Lynton, E. A., and Elman, S. E. *New Priorities for the University: Meeting Society's Needs for Applied Knowledge and Competent Individuals.* San Francisco: Jossey-Bass, 1987.

Pelikan, J. *The Idea of the University: A Reexamination.* New Haven, Conn.: Yale University Press, 1992.

Queen's University. *A Commitment to Excellence: Report of a Task Force on Graduate Studies and Research in the Humanities and the Social Sciences.* London, Ontario: Queen's University, 1975.

Schön, D. A. *The Reflective Practitioner: How Professionals Think in Action.* New York: Basic Books, 1983.

Senge, P. *The Fifth Discipline: The Art and Practice of the Learning Organization.* New York: Doubleday, 1991.

Swenson, C. D. *Teaching Goals of Practitioner–Educators: Increasing Reflective Practice in Higher Education.* Unpublished doctoral dissertation, Walden University, 1995.

Verduin, Jr., J. R., and Clark, T. A. *Distance Education: The Foundations of Effective Practice.* San Francisco: Jossey-Bass, 1991.

Watkins, K. E., and Marsick, V. J. *Sculpting the Learning Organization: Lessons in the Art and Science of Systematic Change.* San Francisco: Jossey-Bass, 1993.

Whittington, N. "Is Instructional Television Educationally Effective? A Research Review." *American Journal of Distance Education,* 1987, *1* (1), 47–57.

CRAIG D. SWENSON *is vice president and director of the Utah Campus of the University of Phoenix.*

The author suggests approaches colleges and universities might take as
they address distance education.

Antecedents to Distance Education
and Continuing Education: Time
to Fix Them

Marlowe D. Froke

When the University of Chicago opened in 1892, a former professor of Hebrew
at Yale University with a mission and dedication for correspondence study was
its president. Although the practice of correspondence study had been drawn
earlier from Germany and England, Dr. William Rainey Harper articulated a
unique American adaptation and placed it on the path for individual and
group learning that would lead to the distance education of today. A claim that
he is the father of distance education in the United States is credible. His
accomplishments were visionary and heroic. Further evidence of their historical lineage is the change of name from the International Council on Correspondence Education to the International Council on Distance Education.

   Ironically, today some of Harper's adaptations persist as organizational and
administrative constraints on the development of distance education and other
instructional systems as supplements or alternatives to the classroom system,
or what Harper called the "oral tradition" (Harper, 1990, p. 4). His views of a
century ago remained a part of the culture of higher education with architec-
tural, administrative, and organizational support entrenched in the classroom
system. For instance, Penn State academic policies as late as 1970 included a
provision that no full-time degree student could enroll in a correspondence
course unless he or she had been dropped from the university for academic
reasons. Evidence of satisfactory completion of a correspondence course could
be used as a part of the application for readmission.

   Organizational, administrative, and academic services are the principal
constraints in the adoption of new technologies. They are the real hurdles, not

NEW DIRECTIONS FOR ADULT AND CONTINUING EDUCATION, no. 67, Fall 1995   © Jossey-Bass Publishers

the general slow pace of change or the instructional faculty, immersed in traditional ways of teaching. Faculty are innovative and responsive to appropriate uses of technology for correspondence study, independent learning, and distance education.

Harper Era

Harper prepared his views about correspondence study in the mid 1880s while advancing a system of correspondence for Chautauqua, an important program in the history of university extension and continuing higher education. For Harper, correspondence was a logical organizational structure on which to build formal education as the country responded to the need for new educational institutions and intellectual life in its westward movement. A reliable national mail system was already in place, President Lincoln had signed the Morrill Act of 1862 that set aside land for establishment of a higher education institution in each state, and the British Lyceum movement had spread rapidly across the United States with the people of the individual communities nurturing an intellectual life based on touring outside lecturers and musical and theatrical presentations (Bender, 1994). Chautauqua, even with its religious foundations as a summer camp for Sunday school teachers in Western New York, was central to the secular adult education movement. It remained so until colleges and universities organized to provide general extension and correspondence study, leaving Chautauqua to return slowly to its summer program mission. What Harper prepared for Chautauqua became the organizational foundations for correspondence study.

His concluding paragraph of a statement that defined and listed the advantages and disadvantages of correspondence, as compared to the "oral tradition," was ominous.

> But is any one to suppose that there exists, in the mind of those especially interested in this system, a desire to have it take the place of oral instruction? Is the one in any sense a rival of the other? I wish here to record, in answer to these questions, a most emphatic NO. What is the fact? Only those persons are encouraged to study by correspondence, or, indeed, admitted to such study, who because of age, poverty, occupation situation or some other good reason cannot avail themselves of oral instruction. Away, therefore, with all baseless and foolish prejudice in this matter. The correspondence system would not, if it could, supplant oral instruction, or be regarded as its substitute. There is a field for each which the other cannot fill. Let each do its proper work. [1990, p. 9]

Classroom instruction was placed on a pedestal from which it has not been displaced as the only instructional system in which the encounters of teacher with student and student with student could satisfy the pedagogy of all time. An intervening technology among teachers and students was only a last resort (Hillman, Willis, and Gunawardena, 1994).

Follow the Leader

The early characterizations and decisions at Chicago had dire consequences for correspondence study there and elsewhere. Antagonism mounted as the years passed. Faculty participation waned and enrollments declined. Chicago eventually closed its correspondence program in 1933.

Similarly traumatic were the early years of correspondence at other colleges and universities. The University of Wisconsin, for instance, closed its first program, then revived it in the early 1890s with a practical and vocational emphasis. It went on to become one of the nation's leaders in distance education, strongly supported by the university and the political and governmental structure, undoubtedly as a reflection of the progressive history of the state (Carstensen, 1990).

Unfortunately, those early years were influenced by Harper's perspectives. An 1891 catalog baldly proclaimed: "The correspondence system is inferior to the lecture and class system in that it lacks the personal supervision and inspiration which are so important factors in the best educations but has compensating merit of being adopted to a sparse population and to special students who cannot gather themselves into classes or audiences to receive lectures and personal instruction" (Watkins, 1991, p. 12).

In a sense, Harper and other leaders of individual colleges and universities simply reflected priorities of the country. Public policy that led to tax-supported education for children and youth did not evolve to include adults, except in agriculture and home economics. Financing for adult education at all levels was provided only on a special project basis, with limited appropriations at both the national and state levels. Even at times of crises such as the Great Depression and World War II, support for correspondence study in the Civilian Conservation Corps and United States Armed Forces Institute was anecdotal, despite their scope, scale, and success.

Rhetoric about the need for adult education has been constant over the past century, repeating the same themes. When the University of Wisconsin convened in 1915 the first national meeting of university continuing education leaders, its president, Charles Van Hise, opened the two-day conference with words that have echoed to the present day:

> To about the middle of the nineteenth century the advancement of knowledge was comparatively slow, and at least a fair proportion of the knowledge that the people could apply had been assimilated by them in the more enlightened nations. But since the year 1850 the advancement of knowledge has been greater than in a thousand and probably in five thousand years before. The result is that the accumulation of knowledge has far outrun the assimilation of the people. Much of this knowledge has accumulated during the past twenty-five years, since men still in full maturity have left the schools and colleges. [Van Hise, 1991, p. 20]

Although specific appropriations and patterns for financing agriculture and home economics extension came in 1914 with the passage of the Smith-Lever Act, financial support for other academic disciplines did not emerge until the 1950s, culminating with passage in 1965 of Title I of the Higher Education Act (U.S. Statutes at Large, Vol. 79, 1965). Funds were allocated to the individual states for the support of lifelong learning, a term used a century earlier at Chautauqua. Allocations to the states were minor. Even so, appropriations for Title I were discontinued in 1981. Tax credits as a means of reducing the financial impact on adults did get on the table again in the 1991 federal budget deliberations.

The priority of adult students in higher education has been limited further by interpretations at the federal and state levels of their eligibility as part-time students. Into the 1970s, there were also limitations on the use of the funds for nonclassroom instructional systems, specifically correspondence.

Technology Perspective

Distance education is a term that conveys an impression of ever-increasing technological resources for organizing, presenting, and disseminating knowledge. The centuries-old evolution of these resources has been dominated by writing and printing. These technologies have determined the nature of interaction among learners. The classroom became the physical base for encounters of students and teachers and the organization and administration of educational institutions. Now, electronic technologies, which contributed to bringing the term *distance education* into favor in the United States, are showing an awesome potential for all educational functions (instruction, research, and service) as well as academic and administrative services. Their impact on education and all other institutions is pervasive in producing change, with resulting benefits and new concerns ("Technology and Unemployment," 1995).

These technologies expand access to educational resources worldwide. They stimulate reform and renewal by requiring new perspectives on teaching and learning. They provide opportunities to better serve existing students and thereby contribute to an institution's ability to expand its services to older adult students. Most telling of the changes ahead are remarks by the president of the American Association of State Colleges and Universities. James P. Appleberry noted that "private commercial ventures will establish themselves as large electronic data bases, and that these will compete with and—perhaps in some cases—supplant university libraries" (1995, p. 1). On the other hand, librarians were among the first to sign on for the information revolution, embracing computer technology in numerous major projects to convert card catalogs to data. The Internet is no stranger to libraries. Maryland librarians took the lead in getting state appropriations to issue e-mail addresses to library users.

However, there are manifestations of Appleberry's prediction. IBM Digital, for instance, entered into a partnership in 1995 with the Vatican Library to convert its holdings to digital form (Lohr, 1995). Earlier, IBM had signed agreements with Indiana University and the Los Angeles Public Library. Except for the need for additional refinements for user access of the Internet, similar data bases are in place and expanding in volume, quality, and number. *The Smithsonian* and *The New York Times*, two traditions in research and informal education, are now services of America Online. *The Wall Street Journal,* the *Washington Post,* and the *Los Angeles Times,* three other newspapers widely used in education, can also be read from the Internet.

The early commercial data bases—Compuserve, America Online, Prodigy, and Delphi, each with one million customers by 1995—saw newcomers such as Netcom complement the service array or directly compete ("Delphi Internet to Expand," 1995; "Netcom Names a President," 1995). In 1995, Pacific Bell and MCI announced plans for enhanced services on the Internet (Lewis, 1995b). By 1995, the Internet reached 4.5 million computers: 3.2 million in the United States and the remainder in 159 other nations. Additional networks are connecting to the Internet at the rate of one every twenty-two seconds ("Internet," 1995).

To enhance the use of the Internet, Stanford University and five other universities have attempted to find ways for users to work with an on-line card catalog, making it easier to find things and eliminating characterizations of the Internet as a Tower of Babel (Langberg, 1995). With similar goals in mind, new software programs and technology for navigating the Internet have moved on-line, including World Wide Web, Netscape, Mosaic, Netcom Netcruiser, IBM WebExplorer, Gopher, and the MBONE (Lewis, 1995a). By 1995, the Internet could communicate as a unicast (one-to-one), broadcast (one-to-many) and multicast (many-to-many) ("Internet Users Peer Out . . .," 1995).

Demonstrating the ever-increasing adaptations and use of technology, entrepreneurs through MBONE used substantial amounts of the Internet's bandwidth to transmit a blues concert on January 18, 1995, as part of a tribute to Martin Luther King. As a multicast, it could go to only a limited number of computers ("I Got the MBONE Blues," 1995). The stage has been set for telecommunications to broaden its portrayal of culture by including film, video, theater, and other performing arts with a technical quality that would satisfy most mass audiences. To improve the development of video distribution on the Internet, an old technology that seemed to be going nowhere in the United States has come back in favor: Integrated Services Digital Network (Cochenour, 1994; "Technology," 1995).

Like technology itself, the Internet is becoming pervasive. Included in its reach are information resources through files and networks that can serve education in formal and informal ways. Browsing the Internet might well be the twenty-first-century equivalent of the Lyceums and Chautauqua, a new base for enhancing on-campus education, and the beginning of a new era in adult education. SeniorNet is ready to become the twenty-first-century equivalent of the elderhostel, which in the last three decades has brought intellectual stimulation to older Americans through travel to the nation's college and university campuses.

Other Precursors of Distance Education

Every college and university already has the technology to participate in the information age to one degree or another. It can begin with nothing more complicated than a speaker telephone and a telephone jack in a classroom. To the students of that class and the teacher, the world is available for conversations with political leaders, scientists, and faculty at other institutions. It can also begin with the library taking on a full-range of acquisition and storage, at individual faculty requests and within acquisition budgets, of audiotapes, videotapes, and disciplinary computer programs for use in courses. The librarian of the institution can also be asked to encourage academic disciplines to systematically evaluate nonprint instructional materials that might be acquired for use in on- and off-campus settings.

Distance education could also begin with purchase of a low-cost video camera to focus on a conventional classroom course. It could be connected by a local telecommunications vendor to a location off-campus where other registered students are assembled. The only difference is that they are further away from the faculty member and their student colleagues. Distance education could also begin with a single faculty member working at home, communicating two-way by keyboard with the students using conventional telephone lines.

All of these low-tech approaches to distance education are now in use, as are more high-tech approaches that grew from low-tech beginnings. Today, their statistics are individually impressive, but in the national aggregate, compared to the classroom instructional design that firmly dominates colleges and universities, relatively insignificant.

Almost 350,000 students are enrolled at about 1,900 colleges and universities in the United States in courses available through the PBS Adult Learning Services ("Missing Link . . .," 1995).

Students from Clemson, Georgia Institute of Technology, Johns Hopkins University, University of Nebraska, University of Delaware, and Stevens Institute of Technology are connected to Penn State students for lectures from experts from the University of Newcastle, the Indian Institute of Science, AT&T Bell Labs, and the Swiss Federal Institute of Technology ("Students Connected . . .," 1995).

More than 3,000 hours of instruction and 600 meetings have been conducted over a telecommunications network of Texas A & M for delivery at twenty cities and thirty-two sites (Ryan, 1995).

The Georgia Center for Continuing Education is linked to the Georgia Statewide Academic and Medical System Network of two-way compressed video sites for delivery of continuing education programs to the state ("Center Completes New Instructional Studio," 1995).

Regents College, the University of the State of New York, offers twenty-six associate and baccalaureate degrees in liberal arts, business, nursing, and technology, serving more than 16,000 students every year. Approximately 4,000 students have graduated each year (Regents College, 1994).

National Technological University, Fort Collins, Colorado, has become the largest source of continuing education for engineers ("Different Organizations and Agencies . . .," 1995).

SeniorNet has been created for adults fifty-five years of age and older. With more than 14,000 members and 60 learning centers, SeniorNet offers computer books, software, and accessories to help older adults explore the on-line world.

In other countries, examples include British Open University, with twenty-five years of operation, which has enrolled 135,000 students in degree courses and another 100,000 in others; The University of South Africa, the oldest of the open universities patterned after the British Open University, to which Nelson Mandela enrolled while he was in prison; Central China Television University, which has an estimated 1–2 million students; and Mind Extension University, based in Colorado, which has extended its distance education courses to Taiwan and plans to open in Thailand ("Different Organizations . . .," 1995).

The Economist reports that the University of Alabama had to caution an estimated 60,000 people, who came for a course on the Internet, not to call in because it would overload the computer ("Different Organizations . . .," 1995).

Independent study enrollments in institutions that are members of the National University Continuing Education Association reached 391,789 in 1992–1993 (Independent Study Division, 1992–1993).

TI-IN Network, Carrollton, Texas, offers live, interactive programming by satellite to schools across the nation. Subject areas include mathematics, science, and foreign languages.

Others could be cited, some of equal scope and scale, and some with intriguing titles such as The Indiana Academy, The School Districts of Philadelphia Network, The Hispanic Informational and Telecommunications Network, and the Miami/Dade Network, all listed in the 1995–1996 Program Guide of the Distance Learning Associates.

Factors in Growth

The growth of distance education is the result of technological advances in the distribution of data, voice, and video. In the United States, growth has been stimulated by federal communications policy that encouraged competition among cable television, AT&T, the seven regional Bell operating companies, Sprint, and MCI, all moving toward a level playing field for local and long-distance service. Distribution of instructional services has been enhanced by the competition. Still more is being planned by federal administrative agencies and Congress (Andrews, 1995).

Business alliances and mergers to provide a competitive edge are widespread ("Technology Trends in the Cable Industry," 1995). All are promising data, voice, and video on demand, including the newest arrival, a consortium of Bell Atlantic, Nynex, and Pacific Telesis (Carter, 1995). Other competitors are being added as new technologies move to national systems in personal communications. By 1995, more than 25 million wireless telephones had been sold (Naik, 1995).

A rapidly expanding Internet, the ad hoc telecommunications highway that emerged from the joint needs of the military, government, and academic researchers, now serves a much wider range of applications, including commerce and entertainment. Its status has been improved with sophisticated protocols and supporting resources. Meanwhile, telecommunications vendors and software developers seek alignments to provide competitive responses. Their ability to respond for local, long-distance, and international services was strengthened in February 1995 by agreements among the United States and six other key industrial nations to apply free-market principles to global communications. Other nations were expected to join later in the year (Nash, 1995).

The "getting there and back" part of distance education has technologically far outstripped the capability of its use by the higher education institutions, although within each progress is being made to develop economical and effective internal media and telecommunications capabilities for students, faculty, and staff. They are renting, leasing, or constructing microwave, satellite, coaxial cable, and fiberoptics to create the expanded electronic space necessary for transmission of the various formats. A dramatic development in Pennsylvania was an appropriation of $15 million by the General Assembly to Penn State to improve its internal telecommunications infrastructure. That will be added to a satellite system of two uplinks and almost fifty downlinks; its public television and public radio stations, which are moving to capitalize on the impact of digital technology in telecommunications; a statewide cable network with distribution by microwave, fiber, and satellite; two-way T-1 links between the main University Park campus and four of its other campuses; and more than 46,000 faculty, student, and staff accounts for Internet access ("Gridlock on the Internet," 1995).

Conclusion

Despite its progress, higher education is merely scratching the surface in its application of existing technology. At a pragmatic level, for instance, it is logical that the communications technologies should lead to adjustments in system budgeting that reflected modified or new roles for teachers and learners. Rarely has this occurred. The need is there and agreed to but no end is in sight to the practices of adding costs of the technology to the existing costs of the classroom instructional design.

Rising costs have squeezed the ability of students, parents, and government to pay fees, whether for resident or distance education (DeLoughry, 1995). Adjustments to reflect cost savings from the appropriate use of the technology have not been made. Instead, institutions have continued to turn to fee increases and conventional cost-saving measures that sometimes cut to the heart of intellectual life. Distance education has continued to build on the shaky foundations of ad hoc financial strategies that came from the Harper era and even then were alien to high-quality education. It is not enough to view distance education as a phenomenon that in time will simply be absorbed or assimilated in the on-going organizational systems of the institution. One hundred years of experience in correspondence study and other precursors of distance education have shown the need to position distance education with the individual academic units and their faculty, where the definition of a course could become not only the content but also an appropriate instructional design. We desperately need well-planned, integrated administrative practices and systematic processes for transition from almost total emphasis on the classroom instructional design to new designs that use appropriately the new technologies and take into account their awesome social implications.

Most pressing is a vision for media and telecommunications that reflects more closely human needs and the potential of technology. A coherent long-term strategy for most colleges and universities has yet to be realized (Saba, 1994). It is time to study again the imperfections of the correspondence model of William Rainey Harper and finally move distance education under the main tent of higher education.

References

Andrews, E. L. "U.S. Plans More Phone Competition." *New York Times,* March 1, 1995, p. D2.

Independent Study Division. *Annual Report.* Washington, D.C.: National University Continuing Education Association, 1992–1993.

Appleberry, J. W. "The Virtual University." *Five Minutes with ACHE, the Newsletter of the American Association for Continuing Higher Education,* Feb. 1995, pp. 1, 4.

Bender, T. "The Cultures of Intellectual Life." *Kettering Review,* Winter 1994, pp. 46–52.

Carstensen, V. W. "Educational Service—The Wisconsin Idea." In R. W. Rohfeld (ed.), *Expanding Access to Knowledge: Continuing Higher Education.* Washington, D.C.: National University Continuing Education Association, 1990.

Carter, B. "Stringer Leaves CBS Broadcast Job." *New York Times,* Feb. 24, 1995, pp. D1, D2.

"Center Completes New Instructional Studio." *Five Minutes with ACHE, the Newsletter of the Association for Continuing Higher Education,* Jan. 1995, p. 4.

Cochenour, J. "Mosaic: A Hypertext Tool for Navigating the Internet." *American Journal of Distance Education,* 1994, 8 (2), 80–83.

DeLoughry, T. J. "Steep Increase in Satellite Costs Concerns Colleges." *Chronicle of Higher Education,* March 17, 1995, p. A21.

"Delphi Internet to Expand." *New York Times,* March 1, 1995, p. D6.

"Different Organizations and Agencies Offering Distance Learning." *Economist,* Jan. 7, 1995, pp. 53–54.

"Gridlock on the Internet." *Penn State INTERCOM,* March 16, 1995, pp. 1, 5.

Harper, W. R. "On Teaching by Correspondence." In R. W. Rohfeld (ed.), *Expanding Access to Knowledge: Continuing Higher Education.* Washington, D.C.: National University Continuing Education Association, 1990.

Hillman, D.C.A., Willis, D. J., and Gunawardena, C. N. "Learner-Interface Interaction in Distance Education: An Extension of Contemporary Models and Strategies for Practitioners." *American Journal of Distance Education,* 1994, 8 (2), 30–42.

"I Got the MBONE Blues." *Wired,* March 1995, p. 41.

"Internet." *U.S. News & World Report,* Feb. 27, 1995, p. 14.

"Internet Users Peer Out a 'Real Time' Window." *New York Times,* Feb. 8, 1995, p. D7.

Langberg, M. "Stanford Developing Efficient Internet 'Bus.'" *Centre Daily Times,* Feb. 23, 1995, p. 10B.

Lewis, P. H. "Netscape Knows Fame and Aspires to Fortune." *New York Times,* March 1, 1995a, p. D1.

Lewis, P. H. "Pacific Bell, MCI to Expand Internet Service." *New York Times,* March 28, 1995b, p. D3.

Lohr, S. "I.B.M. and Vatican Library Team Up for a This-Worldly Project." *New York Times,* March 28, 1995, p. D3.

"Missing Link: Finding Ways to Teach Speech at a Distance." *Current,* Feb. 20, 1995, p. 11.

Naik, G. "Craig O. McCaw Confounds the Giants with His Wild and Wooly PCS Bidding." *Wall Street Journal,* Feb. 23, 1995, p. B1.

Nash, N. C. "Group of 7 Defines Policies About Telecommunications." *New York Times,* Feb. 27, 1995, p. D1.

"Netcom Names a President." *New York Times,* March 1, 1995, p. D6.

Regents College, the University of the State of New York, promotional flyer, 1994.

Ryan, J. H. "Distance Education: An Idea Whose Time Has Come." Presented at the Graduate Program in Nutrition Colloquium, University Park, Pa., Spring 1995.

Saba, F. "The Information Superhighway." *American Journal of Distance Education,* 1994, *8* (3), 84–87.

"Students Connected to Other College's Faculty." *Daily Collegian,* Jan. 29, 1995, p. 1.

"Technology." *Economist,* Jan. 7, 1995, pp. 54–55.

"Technology Trends in the Cable Industry." *From the Source, A Newsletter for Participants of Cable '95, Dallas, Tex.,* 1995, *8* (2), 1–10.

"Technology and Unemployment." *Economist,* Feb. 1995, pp. 21–23.

U.S. Statutes at Large, Vol. 79, 1219–1224. *Higher Education Act of 1965, Title I—Community Service and Continuing Education Programs,* 1965.

Van Hise, C. "The University Extension Function in the Modern University." In R. W. Rohfeld (ed.), *Expanding Access to Knowledge: Continuing Higher Education.* Washington, D.C.: National University Continuing Education Association, 1991.

Watkins, B. L. "A Quite Radical Idea: The Invention and Elaboration of Collegiate Correspondence Study." In B. L. Watkins and S. J. Wright (eds.), *The Foundations of American Distance Education.* Dubuque, Iowa: Kendall/Hunt, 1991.

MARLOWE D. FROKE *is retired as general manager emeritus and associate professor of communications emeritus, Pennsylvania State University.*

*This chapter identifies on-line pathways that make finding new
courses, recent publications, on-going discussions of issues, and other
resources more effective and efficient for the distance educator.*

Distance Learning Resources for Distance Educators

Sherrill Weaver

Bibliographers of distance education, notably Jill H. Ellsworth and Keith W.
Harry, continue to provide articles, electronic files, and books that list various
resources of interest to distance educators pursuing continuing professional
education. These lists, especially Ellsworth's *Education on the Internet: A Hands-
on Book of Ideas, Resources, Projects, and Advice* (1994) and Harry's "A Rough
Guide to Distance Education Journals and Newsletters" (1994), map the print
and electronic features of the terrain of distance education. Each is indispens-
able for the coverage it provides of a literature that spans media boundaries.
Whereas Harry deftly captures the ephemeral literature of newsletters,
Ellsworth collects an extensive chapter of distance education resource electronic addresses. Harry and Ellsworth's ongoing works exemplify the best of
both the traditional print bibliographic approach to publications and the electronic bibliographic approach to addresses (FTP or other file transfer, Gopher
directory, worldwide web home page) to electronically presented materials.
Together, these bibliographies form a topography of distance education with
electronic rivers and forests of information as the terrain and citations to print
publications as the cities and towns dotting the landscape.

As useful as these bibliographies are in identifying specific citations and
general areas of information, they don't show paths between these two types
of resources, paths that make finding new courses, recent publications, and
ongoing discussions more effective and efficient for the distance educator. This
chapter seeks to chart those paths and to suggest ways in which trails can be
found or cleared to link resources together in a route that distance educators
can travel periodically to keep current in research, technological innovation,
and conference topics. From this pathfinder, an educator can select paths that

lead to sites of specific research or practice interests. People with the computer capability to access graphic interfaces, such as worldwide web sites, can contact the Gopher sites listed for new WWW addresses.

Path to the Literature of Distance Education

Contribution to and critical consumption of research are the most common activities in professional continuing education. Distance education praxis benefits from the existence of international and national data bases that effectively encompass the literature of the field. Fortunately, two of these data bases, the International Centre for Distance Learning (ICDL) and the Educational Resources Information Center, are readily available at Internet addresses and Gopher sites.

International Centre for Distance Learning. International coverage of journal articles, conference proceedings, and organization reports is provided by ICDL, based at the United Kingdom Open University. Well-organized and conveniently constructed to include an efficient interface for downloading entries to e-mail files, the ICDL data base offers an international gateway to distance education literature, courses, and institutions.

ICDL can be accessed via Internet connection to acsvax.open.ac.uk. At the USERNAME prompt, type *ICDL*. At the COUNTRY prompt, type the country three-letter identification code *USA*. At the PASSWORD prompt, type *AAA*. Select terminal type VT100.

The Gopher address for ICDL is rowan.open.ac.uk at port 70. (If you have any questions about connecting to ICDL, contact Nazira Ismail at n.ismail @open.ac.uk. For answers to questions about the data base contents, contact Keith Harry, Director, International Centre for Distance Learning at The Open University, Walton Hall, Milton Keynes MK7 6AA or k.w.harry@open.ac.uk.)

In the ICDL literature section, the data base is divided into subject areas. These subject areas encompass distance education theory, policy, access, development, application, program aspects, student characteristics, student support, curriculum, instruction, and institutional administration. Literature searches originate with keyword searches conducted in a given subject area. These subject areas can be chosen from a hierarchical array of broader and narrower subjects. Submenus of narrower terms under each broad subject area provide a convenient hierarchical scheme of subject headings that effectively divide discipline areas. Within this hierarchy, a search can be limited by author, title, or publication year.

All subject areas can be queried at once in a search. By combining subject headings and keywords, users can conduct effective cross-disciplinary searches. Despite the constraints of the hierarchy of broad and narrow subject divisions, finding interrelationships among separate areas of research is feasible because indexing terms that relate the document to other divisions in the subject hierarchy are added to each entry. Thus, consistent and reliable indexing allows for keyword topic searches across subjects.

In addition to finding studies in particular subject areas or on selected topics, educators who regularly search ICDL as a stop along their continuing education route will find the print journal table of contents and on-line journal full-text features especially useful. Current awareness of research topics in key publications can easily be achieved by browsing these sections of the data base.

Educational Resources Information Center. Some of the publications indexed in ICDL are also indexed in ERIC, which consists of the Current Index to Journals in Education and Resources in Education. The overlap of indexing should not preclude searches in ERIC, for this data base provides comprehensive international coverage of educational print resources. ERIC can be accessed at two sites.

One site for ERIC access is located at the University of Iowa at oasis.uiowa.edu at port 23. Select "?" and then choose the appropriate terminal type. At the main menu, choose 1. Oasis; in the Oasis menu, type *INDEXES.* At the next screen, type *ERIC.* The interface at this connection resembles an online library catalog with both brief (citation only) and long (all fields including the abstract) views available. On-line help screens for author, title, subject, and keyword searches can be accessed at each screen.

An alternative address for the ERIC data base is sklib.usask.ca (128.233.1.20). Log in as eric. The University of Saskatchewan supports its search interface with an on-line tutorial and help screens. Citations can be viewed in the scan mode, and all fields (citations and abstracts) appear in the full mode.

ERIC indexes an extensive collection of lesson plans, course outlines, conference proceedings, and educational reports as well as indexed journal articles published over the past twenty years. Searching ERIC is especially effective for locating distance education demonstration project descriptions and for identifying national government plans for distance education delivery systems. Many U.S. state reports on the planning and implementation of statewide telecommunication and computer networks also can be found in ERIC. These local, state, and national documents are valuable as planning process outlines and product reports. ERIC also provides access to regional U.S. distance education conference proceedings.

Most ERIC documents are readily available through the ERIC Document Reproduction Service (EDRS) or University Microfilms International (UMI) delivery services. For information about EDRS call (800) 443–3742 or (703) 440–1400 (or EDRS, 7420 Fullerton Road, Suite 110, Springfield, VA 22153–2852). UMI can be contacted at (800) 521–0600, ext. 2786 or (313) 665–7075 (or UMI, Article Clearinghouse, 300 North Zeeb Road, P.O. Box 1346, Ann Arbor, MI 48106–1346).

ERIC search assistance is offered to educators through AskERIC. For more information about AskERIC services, send a query to askeric@ericir.syr.edu. or call (800) 464–9107 or (315) 443–3640 (or ERIC Clearinghouse on Information & Technology, Syracuse University, Syracuse, NY 13244–2340). The clearinghouse at Syracuse University compiles reports in its *ERIC Digests;* these can be especially useful for finding more resources accessible through the Internet.

OCLC First Search. Although both ICDL and ERIC also provide some access to book reviews, OCLC searches provide for a timely notice of recent monograph publications. Access to OCLC is restricted to paid subscribers, but most U.S. libraries subscribe and many make this data base available to patrons through the FirstSearch interface. Distance educators who make arrangements through a local or university library for periodic searches can quickly update the bibliographies previously mentioned. When requesting a search of OCLC or other national cataloging data base, include publishers' names as regular search terms combined with terms for distance education. The following publishers support monographic series that include titles in distance education: Kogan Page, Routledge, Cassell, Hampton Press, The Commonwealth of Learning, Open Learning Institute Press (Hong Kong), Open University Press (UK), Jossey-Bass, and The American Center for the Study of Distance Education.

Path to Course Offerings and Institutional Development in Distance Education

Updating skills in educational technology poses a challenge for every distance educator, no matter what level of technology is currently used in the course they instruct. Traditional correspondence education is being rapidly altered by e-mail use, and satellite and fiberoptic transmissions of sound, pictures, and data are revolutionizing traditional televised instruction. Keeping skills current and maintaining awareness of developments in new technology can be achieved through frequent browsing or searching in the National Distance Learning Center (NDLC), the University of Wisconsin Clearinghouse for Distance Education, the Institute for Academic Technology, and the ICDL courses data bases.

National Distance Learning Center. The NDLC data base was established to collect detailed listings of courses for elementary through postsecondary learners. The course descriptions are submitted by course providers. The NDLC offers electronic space in this data base in which providers may advertise courses free of charge in order to facilitate widespread dissemination of distance education opportunities.

The address for the Internet connection to NDLC is ndlc.occ.uky.edu, with the login ndlc (an opening screen requesting user information must be filled out before the data base becomes accessible for searching). To obtain a user's guide to NDLC, contact (502) 686–4556 (or National Distance Learning Center, Owensboro Community College, University of Kentucky, 4800 New Harford Road, Owensboro, KY 42303).

The NCDL offers course listings searchable by provider, medium, subject, audience, and date under two separate data base divisions, correspondence and distance learning. This division by delivery system, useful before the widespread use of computer-mediated communication, now inhibits rather than enhances searching this data base because these categories are no longer entirely distinct. For example, listed among correspondence courses are those that include e-mail as a correspondence delivery system, whereas the distance learning section lists computer-mediated courses, which also include e-mail as a delivery system.

However, other features of the data base are more advantageous. The pre-coordinated search categories facilitate frequent searches for educators whose parameters of delivery medium, provider, subject, or audience remain unchanged. The same combination of provider and subject or subject and audience, for example, can be searched periodically to update a calendar of professional continuing education experiences from which to choose.

University of Wisconsin Extension: Distance Education Clearinghouse. The University of Wisconsin Extension supports the Distance Education Clearinghouse, which may be accessed through Gopher connection.

The Distance Education Clearinghouse brings together a variety of providers who offer credit and noncredit programs and lists them in an alphabetical table of contents. Included among the credit course providers is the University of Wisconsin, which offers a Certificate of Professional Development in Distance Education through its Department of Continuing and Vocational Education. The clearinghouse provides a description of the program and identifies the source for more information about the coursework; call (608) 262–8530 or contact UW-Madison, Department of Continuing and Vocational Education, 225 N. Mills Street, Room 112, Madison, WI 53708. In addition to course information, the clearinghouse also lists distance education funding sources by type and by application deadline.

Institute for Academic Technology. Formed by the convergence of higher education and corporate training interests, the Institute for Academic Technology (IAT) brings together the resources of the University of North Carolina at Chapel Hill and the IBM Corporation to support the development of continuing education in instructional technologies. Information about IAT seminars (both live and videotaped) can be requested by message to info.iat@mhs.unc.edu (or IAT Events, 2525 Meridian Parkway, Suite 400, Durham, NC 27713).

ICDL: Courses. ICDL's main menu offers *courses* as a selection choice that leads to degree and credit courses offered by a host of institutions, many of them in Australia, Canada, India, Hong Kong, and the United Kingdom.

Course outlines included in this section of the ICDL data base are detailed and some indicate that many degrees, including graduate and postgraduate, can be earned completely through distance education. Searches for courses can be conducted in a variety of subject areas, including vocational (such as agriculture), professional (such as law), and academic (such as pure science). The hierarchical structure of the ICDL data base, with its broad and narrow subject headings, remains as effective in this course section as it is in the literature section.

Paths to News, Organizations, and Discussions in Distance Education

On-line connections to newsletters, journals, organizations, associations, listservers, and discussion groups are available to distance educators through subscription to Internet resources. Although distance education theoretically is global, the origination and coverage of newsletters reveals the political geography of the field.

Three lists of listservers cover the discussion groups of most interest to distance educators. These are "Distance Education: Electronic Sources for Information and Discussion" compiled by Carolyn Kotlas (access through IBM Kiosk for Education, or IKE), the "9th Revision of Scholarly Electronic Conferences" compiled by Diane Kovacs and the Directory Team (see access information for Arizona State University), and "Dr. E's Compendium of Electronic Resources of Adult/Distance Education," compiled by Jill Ellsworth, which is available through the Distance Education Clearinghouse at the University Wisconsin Extension.

The Ellsworth and Kotlas directories offer access to the same listservers, which originate in the United States, Canada, Australia, and South America. The difference between the two directories lies in their coverage of additional resources. Ellsworth provides addresses for electronic refereed journals, newsletters, and bulletin boards. Kotlas extends her list to include bibliographies of subjects such as user interface design.

The third directory, compiled by Diane Kovacs and the Directory Team, is an authoritative source for subject or discipline area listservers that present discussions about distance education issues in the context of related educational or scholarly concerns.

Pathfinding

Organizing a process for systematic review of distance education resources requires time for exploration and evaluation of resources. Selecting from among available Gopher sites, listserver discussion groups, and on-line and print journals and newsletters is time-consuming. Four educational Gophers provide ready-made pathways to essential resources for professional continuing education for distance educators.

Arizona State University. Arizona State University, accessible via Gopher to info.asu.edu at port 70, lists education resources by institution, publication, and agency. This Gopher hosts a link to the Kovacs academic listserver directory. It also includes links to college and university departments of education, research collections, electronic journals, higher education organizations, K–12 districts and resources, association publications, government agencies, educational technology projects, and other subject Gophers. Questions about the ASU Gopher can be addressed to Gene V. Glass at glass@asu.edu (or Division of Leadership and Policy Studies, College of Education, Arizona State University, Tempe, AZ 85287–2411 or (602) 965–2692).

IBM Kiosk for Education. IKE is accessible by Gopher connection to ike.engr.washington.edu at port 70. This Gopher houses IAT, which includes the Kotlas listserver directory as well as on-line newsletters and technical papers. IKE also hosts IBM company and product information for PC users. More information about IKE is available at ike@ike.engr.washington.edu or (206) 543–5604.

Rice University. Rice University distance education resources are accessible by Gopher connection to gopher.rice.edu at port 70. The Rice University

Gopher displays an alphabetical rather than categorical menu. This nonhierarchical directory permits easy access to resources by name. Despite its length of twenty-one screens, this menu efficiently facilitates connections to a large variety of resources including the ERIC, ICDL, and NDLC data bases, as well as the Ellsworth listserver. Questions about this Gopher can be addressed to riceinfo@rice.edu or to the Consulting Center at (713) 527–4983.

University of Wisconsin Extension. The University of Wisconsin Extension Gopher connection is gopher.uwex.edu at port 70. At the opening menu, the Distance Education Clearinghouse, a comprehensive list of statewide resources, can be selected. At the national and international level, the clearinghouse lists newsletters, journals, professional groups, course providers, conference announcements, calls for papers, and full-text journal issues. Additionally, order forms for monographs, funding guides, print journals, and audio productions relating to distance education are presented for convenient downloading or printing.

Information about the clearinghouse can be obtained from Instructional Communications Systems at (608) 262–3465 or from Marcia Baird at baird@ics.uwex.edu (or Marcia Baird, Director, Instructional Communications Systems, University of Wisconsin-Extension, 975 Observatory Drive, Madison, WI 53706).

Mapmaking

Mapping the first route to resources in distance education is a critical step to successful continuing education. The pathfinding Gopher sites listed above are excellent starting points. Once paths are selected, routes can be mapped and travelled as often as necessary to stay up-to-date.

References

Ellsworth, J. H. *Education on the Internet: A Hands-on Book of Ideas, Resources, Projects, and Advice.* Indianapolis: Sams Publishing, 1994.

Harry, K. W. "A Rough Guide to Distance Education Journals and Newsletters." *Open Praxis,* 1994, *1,* 6–9.

SHERRILL WEAVER *is Walden University library liaison, Indiana University.*

INDEX

Accreditation, 7

Adult learners: Chatauqua program for, 3, 42, 62; demographic/economic changes and, 51–52; organizational learning and, 51; professional requirements of, 51; special needs of, 51, 53–54; technological changes and, 51–52; telecourses for, 43–44; work force demographics and, 51–52. *See also* Students

Adults: learning of, 36–37; older, 37; SeniorNet for, 37, 65

Anderson, C. W., 52

Andrews, E. L., 67

Annenberg/Corporation for Public Broadcasting (CPB) Project, 44

Appleberry, J. W., 64

Arizona State University, 76

AT&T Learning Network, 15

Babich, A. M., 22

Baird, M. A., 52

Ball State University (Ind.), 15

Barron, A. E., 24

Bates, M., 21

Beatty, T. R., 15

Bender, T., 62

Billings, D., 23

Blank, W. E., 20, 22, 23, 28

Boverie, P. E., 23, 24

Bowen, W. G., 52, 55

Briggs, L. J., 25

Brigham Young University, 42–43

British Lyceum movement, 62

Brookfield, S. D., 36, 57

Brown, G., 52

Candy, P. C., 53

Carey, L., 25, 26

Carl, D. R., 15

Carstensen, V. W., 63

Carter, B., 67

Central China Television University, 67

Cercy, S. P., 21

Chancellor's Office Teleducational/Telecommuting Centers, California Community College, 13

Chatauqua program, 3, 42, 62. *See also* Correspondence study

Cherry, C. E., Jr., 20

Clark, T. A., 11, 16, 26, 27, 53, 58

Classroom(s): broadcast, 11; community in, 36; distributed model of, 45–47; Electronic Classroom program, 14–15; two-way broadcast, 11–12

Clouse, R. W., 16, 17

Coast Community College, 43

Cochenour, J., 65

Cognition: assessing, 21; characteristics of, 20; defined, 20

Cognitive style. *See* Learning styles

Coleman, J., 36

Community: buying off of, 34; in classroom, 36; cyberspace and, 35–36; developing sense of, 33; learning approach and, 47–48; meaning of, 33; physical space and, 33–34; technological impact on, 34

Community building: distance education and, 37–39; Internet and, 35–39; Kent State University (example), 33; listserv program and, 38–39; small-group instruction and, 38

Community College Headquarter (Me.), 14

Computer networks/webs: AT&T Learning Network, 15; data bases for, 65; FrEdMail network, 15; Gopher, 65, 71–72; Hispanic Informational and Telecommunications Network, 67; IBM WebExplorer, 65; Integrated Services Digital Network, 65; Internet, 3, 4, 14, 35–39, 47, 64–65, 68; library collections and, 64–65; MBONE, 65; Miami/Dade Network, 67; Mosaic, 65; National Geographic Kids Network, 15; Netcom Netcruiser, 65; Netscape, 65; SANDS, 35; School Net, 14; self-directed learning and, 37; Senior Net, 37, 65; Sociable Web, 35; TI-IN Network, 67; Walden Information Network, 55; Whole Earth 'Lectronic Link, 35; World Wide Web, 65

Computer technology: as destructive, 34; distance learning and, 13–15. *See also* Distance learning technologies

Ordering Information

NEW DIRECTIONS FOR ADULT AND CONTINUING EDUCATION is a series of paperback books that explores issues of common interest to instructors, administrators, counselors, and policy makers in a broad range of adult and continuing education settings—such as colleges and universities, extension programs, businesses, the military, prisons, libraries, and museums. Books in the series are published quarterly in Spring, Summer, Fall, and Winter and are available for purchase by subscription and individually.

SUBSCRIPTIONS for 1995 cost $48.00 for individuals (a savings of 25 percent over single-copy prices) and $64.00 for institutions, agencies, and libraries. Please do not send institutional checks for personal subscriptions. Standing orders are accepted. (For subscriptions outside of North America, add $7.00 for shipping via surface mail or $25.00 for air mail. Orders *must be prepaid* in U.S. dollars by check drawn on a U.S. bank or charged to VISA, MasterCard, or American Express.)

SINGLE COPIES cost $19.00 plus shipping (see below) when payment accompanies order. California, New Jersey, New York, and Washington, D.C., residents please include appropriate sales tax. Canadian residents add GST and any local taxes. Billed orders will be charged shipping and handling. No billed shipments to post office boxes. (Orders from outside North America *must be prepaid* in U.S. dollars by check drawn on a U.S. bank or charged to VISA, MasterCard, or American Express.)

SHIPPING (SINGLE COPIES ONLY): one issue, add $3.50; two issues, add $4.50; three issues, add $5.50; four to five issues, add $6.50; six to seven issues, add $7.50; eight or more issues, add $8.50.

DISCOUNTS FOR QUANTITY ORDERS are available. Please write to the address below for information.

ALL ORDERS must include either the name of an individual or an official purchase order number. Please submit your order as follows:
   Subscriptions: specify series and year subscription is to begin
   Single copies: include individual title code (such as ACE 59)

MAIL ALL ORDERS TO:
   Jossey-Bass Publishers
   350 Sansome Street
   San Francisco, California 94104-1342

FOR SUBSCRIPTION SALES OUTSIDE OF THE UNITED STATES, contact any international subscription agency or Jossey-Bass directly.

OTHER TITLES AVAILABLE IN THE
NEW DIRECTIONS FOR ADULT AND CONTINUING EDUCATION SERIES
Ralph G. Brockett, Editor-in-Chief
Alan B. Knox, Consulting Editor

ACE66 Mentoring: New Strategies and Challenges, *Michael W. Galbraith,
       Norman H. Cohen*
ACE65 Learning Environments for Women's Adult Development:
       Bridges Toward Change, *Kathleen Taylor, Catherine Marienau*
ACE64 Overcoming Resistance to Self-Direction in Adult Learning,
       Roger Hiemstra, Ralph G. Brockett
ACE63 The Emerging Power of Action Inquiry Technologies, *Ann Brooks,
       Karen E. Watkins*
ACE62 Experiential Learning: A New Appproach, *Lewis Jackson,
       Rosemary S. Caffarella*
ACE61 Confronting Racism and Sexism, *Elisabeth Hayes, Scipio A. J. Colin III*
ACE60 Current Perspectives on Administration of Adult Education Programs,
       Patricia Mulcrone
ACE59 Applying Cognitive Learning Theory to Adult Learning,
       Daniele D. Flannery
ACE58 The Adult Educator as Consultant, *Lois J. Zachary, Sally Vernon*
ACE57 An Update on Adult Learning Theory, *Sharan B. Merriam*
ACE56 Rethinking Leadership in Adult and Continuing Education, *Paul J. Edelson*
ACE55 Professionals' Ways of Knowing: New Findings on How to Improve
       Professional Education, *H. K. Morris Baskett, Victoria J. Marsick*
ACE54 Confronting Controversies in Challenging Times: A Call for Action,
       Michael W. Galbraith, Burton R. Sisco
ACE53 Learning for Personal Development, *Lorraine A. Cavaliere, Angela Sgroi*
ACE52 Perspectives on Educational Certificate Programs, *Margaret E. Holt,
       George J. Lopos*
ACE51 Professional Development for Educators of Adults, *Ralph G. Brockett*
ACE50 Creating Environments for Effective Adult Learning, *Roger Hiemstra*
ACE49 Mistakes Made and Lessons Learned: Overcoming Obstacles to Successful
       Program Planning, *Thomas J. Sork*
ACE48 Serving Culturally Diverse Populations, *Jovita M. Ross-Gordon,
       Larry G. Martin, Diane Buck Briscoe*
ACE47 Education Through Community Organizations, *Michael W. Galbraith*
ACE45 Applying Adult Development Strategies, *Mark H. Rossman,
       Maxine E. Rossman*
CE44   Fulfilling the Promise of Adult and Continuing Education,
       B. Allan Quigley
CE43   Effective Teaching Styles, *Elisabeth Hayes*
CE42   Participatory Literacy Education, *Arlene Fingeret, Paul Jurmo*
CE41   Recruiting and Retaining Adult Students, *Peter S. Cookson*
CE32   Issues in Adult Career Counseling, *Juliet V. Miller, Mary Lynne Musgrove*
CE31   Marketing Continuing Education, *Hal Beder*
CE25   Self-Directed Learning: From Theory to Practice, *Stephen Brookfield*
CE22   Designing and Implementing Effective Workshops, *Thomas J. Sork*
CE19   Helping Adults Learn How to Learn, *Robert M. Smith*

UNITED STATES POSTAL SERVICE™

Statement of Ownership, Management, and Circulation
(Required by 39 U.S.C. 3685)

1. Publication Title	2. Publication No.		3. Filing Date
NEW DIRECTIONS FOR ADULT AND CONTINUING EDUCATION	ISSN	1 0 5 2 - 2 8 9 1	9/22/95

4. Issue Frequency	5. No. of Issues Published Annually	6. Annual Subscription Price
Quarterly	Four (4)	$48.00(personal) $64.00(institution)

7. Complete Mailing Address of Known Office of Publication *(Street, City, County, State, and ZIP+4) (Not Printer)*

350 Sansome Street, 5th Floor, San Francisco, CA 94104-1342 (San Francisco County)

8. Complete Mailing Address of Headquarters or General Business Office of Publisher *(Not Printer)*

(above address)

9. Full Names and Complete Mailing Addresses of Publisher, Editor, and Managing Editor *(Do Not Leave Blank)*

Publisher *(Name and Complete Mailing Address)*

Jossey-Bass Inc., Publishers (above address)

Editor *(Name and Complete Mailing Address)*

Ralph G. Brockett, Dept of Tech and Adult Educ, Univ of Tennessee, 402 Claxton Addition, Knoxville, TN 37996-3400

Managing Editor *(Name and Complete Mailing Address)*

Lynn D. Luckow, President, Jossey-Bass Inc., Publishers (address above)

10. Owner *(If owned by a corporation, its name and address must be stated and also immediately thereafter the names and addresses of stockholders owning or holding 1 percent or more of the total amount of stock. If not owned by a corporation, the names and addresses of the individual owners must be given. If owned by a partnership or other unincorporated firm, its name and address as well as that of each individual must be given. If the publication is published by a nonprofit organization, its name and address must be stated.) (Do Not Leave Blank.)*

Full Name	Complete Mailing Address
Simon & Schuster, Inc.	PO Box 1172 Englewood Cliffs, NJ 07632-1172

11. Known Bondholders, Mortgagees, and Other Security Holders Owning or Holding 1 Percent or More of Total Amount of Bonds, Mortgages, or Other Securities. If none, check here. ☐ None

Full Name	Complete Mailing Address
same as above	same as above

12. For completion by nonprofit organizations authorized to mail at special rates. *(Check one)* The purpose, function, and nonprofit status of this organization and the exempt status for federal income tax purposes:

☐ Has Not Changed During Preceding 12 Months
☐ Has Changed During Preceding 12 Months
(If changed, publisher must submit explanation of change with this statement)

PS Form 3526, October 1994   *(See Instructions on Reverse)*

---

13. Publication Name	14. Issue Date for Circulation Data Below
NEW DIRECTIONS FOR ADULT AND CONTINUING EDUCATION (ACE)	ACE 65 (Spring 1995)

15. Extent and Nature of Circulation	Average No. Copies Each Issue During Preceding 12 Months	Actual No. Copies of Single Issue Published Nearest to Filing Date
a. Total No. Copies (Net Press Run)	1400	1429
b. Paid and/or Requested Circulation (1) Sales Through Dealers and Carriers, Street Vendors, and Counter Sales (Not Mailed)	208	153
(2) Paid or Requested Mail Subscriptions (Include Advertisers' Proof Copies/Exchange Copies)	752	613
c. Total Paid and/or Requested Circulation (Sum of 15b(1) and 15b(2))	960	766
d. Free Distribution by Mail (Samples, Complimentary, and Other Free)	193	236
e. Free Distribution Outside the Mail (Carriers or Other Means)	0	0
f. Total Free Distribution (Sum of 15d and 15e)	193	236
g. Total Distribution (Sum of 15c and 15f)	1153	1002
h. Copies Not Distributed (1) Office Use, Leftovers, Spoiled	223	427
(2) Return from News Agents	24	0
i. Total (Sum of 15g, 15h(1), and 15h(2))	1400	1429
Percent Paid and/or Requested Circulation (15c / 15g x 100)	83.3%	77%

16. This Statement of Ownership will be printed in the ACE67/Fall 1995 issue of this publication. ☐ Check box if not required to publish.

17. Signature and Title of Editor, Publisher, Business Manager, or Owner   Date

[signature]   Sue Lewis, Director of Periodicals   10-16-95

I certify that all information furnished on this form is true and complete. I understand that anyone who furnishes false or misleading information on this form or who omits material or information requested on the form may be subject to criminal sanctions (including fines and imprisonment) and/or civil sanctions (including multiple damages and civil penalties).

Instructions to Publishers

1. Complete and file one copy of this form with your postmaster on or before October 1, annually. Keep a copy of the completed form for your records.

2. Include in items 10 and 11, in cases where the stockholder or security holder is a trustee, the name of the person or corporation for whom the trustee is acting. Also include the names and addresses of individuals who are stockholders who own or hold 1 percent or more of the total amount of bonds, mortgages, or other securities of the publishing corporation. In item 11, if none, check box. Use blank sheets if more space is required.

3. Be sure to furnish all information called for in item 15, regarding circulation. Free circulation must be shown in items 15d, e, and f.

4. If the publication had second-class authorization as a general or requester publication, this Statement of Ownership, Management, and Circulation must be published; it must be printed in any issue in October or the first printed issue after October, if the publication is not published during October.

5. In item 16, indicate date of the issue in which this Statement of Ownership will be printed.

6. Item 17 must be signed.

Failure to file or publish a statement of ownership may lead to suspension of second-class authorization.

PS Form 3526, October 1994 (Reverse)